Tiny House Living

Book 1:
Comprehensive Beginner's Guide for Newbies

Book 2:
Cardinal Rules for Ditching Your Clutter and Your Mortgage

Book 3:
Essential Strategies for Seasoned Tiny House Dwellers

Michael McCord

Table of Contents

Comprehensive Beginner's Guide for Newbies 5

    Introduction 9

    Chapter 1: Going Tiny 11

    Chapter 2: What is a Tiny House 19

    Chapter 3: Wheels or No? 33

    Chapter 4: The Building 41

    Chapter 5: What to Expect 53

    Chapter 6: Common Mistakes 57

    Chapter 7: Interior Design 63

    Chapter 8: Success Stories 73

    Conclusion 81

Cardinal Rules for Ditching Your Clutter and Your Mortgage 83

    Introduction 87

    Chapter 1: Downsizing within Reason 89

    Chapter 2: The Building Materials 99

    Chapter 3: Off the Grid 105

    Chapter 4: Parking your Tiny House 113

    Chapter 5: Decluttering and Guilt 117

Chapter 6: Organizing Mistakes and Corrections 121

Chapter 7: Testing the Tiny 131

Conclusion 137

Essential Strategies for Seasoned Tiny House Dwellers 139

Introduction 143

Chapter 1: Floor Plans & Design 147

Chapter 2: Financial Considerations of Tiny House Living 153

Chapter 3: Zoning Laws 161

Chapter 4: Building Codes 169

Chapter 5: Maximizing Your Space 173

Chapter 6: Tips & Tricks 185

Chapter 7: Insurance 193

Chapter 8: Tiny Homes Big Communities . 201

Chapter 9: Harmony, Green Living, & Places to Park 209

Conclusion 219

Tiny House Living

Comprehensive Beginner's Guide for Newbies

Copyright 2016- Michael McCord - All rights reserved.

This document is geared towards providing exact and reliable information in regards to the topic and issue covered. The publication is sold with the idea that the publisher is not required to render accounting, officially permitted, or otherwise, qualified services. If advice is necessary, legal or professional, a practiced individual in the profession should be ordered.

- From a Declaration of Principles which was accepted and approved equally by a Committee of the American Bar Association and a Committee of Publishers and Associations.

In no way is it legal to reproduce, duplicate, or transmit any part of this document in either electronic means or in printed format. Recording of this publication is strictly prohibited and any storage of this document is not allowed unless with written permission from the publisher. All rights reserved.

The information provided herein is stated to be truthful and consistent, in that any liability, in terms of inattention or otherwise, by any usage or abuse of any policies, processes, or directions contained within is the solitary and utter responsibility of the recipient reader. Under no circumstances will any legal responsibility or blame be held against the publisher for any reparation, damages, or monetary loss due to the information herein, either directly or indirectly.

Respective authors own all copyrights not held by the publisher.

Introduction

I want to thank you and congratulate you for purchasing Tiny Houses: Comprehensive Beginner's Guide for Newbies.

This book contains proven steps and strategies on how to become an aware and enlightened individual about the pros and cons of the tiny house movement and if it is truly right for you.

Here's an inescapable fact: you will need an open mind and patience, tiny houses do not get built over night.

If you do not want to make living a more simple life a priority, it might in your best interest to accept that a tiny house might not be for you at this particular point in your life.

Additionally, the art of Tiny House Living feeds into the broad spectrum of Real Estate Investing in general. If you are interested in making Real Estate a profitable investment and securing your financial future, we have books that tackle numerous concepts such as **Flipping Houses for Profit**, **Real Estate Investing, Rental Property Investing,** and details on how to embark on a career as a successful **Real Estate Agent**. And we also have a step by step guide to achieving an **excellent Credit Score** to get you a loan with the best rates!!

You can find books on all of these topics- AND MORE- if you visit our Amazon Author page at https://www.amazon.com/-/e/B01LYIFPLO.

If you check out our Real Estate Library, you are guaranteed to profit from Real Estate, Rental Properties, Flipping Houses, and turn this into a lucrative income stream for the rest of your life. Don't miss out!!

But right now let's get back to living tiny. It's time for you to begin building your tiny house and live a big life! So let's read on.

Chapter 1: Going Tiny

Bigger isn't always better. The tiny house movement is a perfect example of this. People around the country are choosing to downgrade from their large homes to a much smaller dwelling, known as a tiny house. Everyone has their own unique reasons for doing so, whether it is because of money, or they just want to reduce their carbon footprint. Whatever, the reason tiny houses have become more and more popular.

Is a tiny house right for you?

If you have been on Instagram, you have probably seen images of people living big in their tiny homes. However, they are not for everyone. If you are considering a tiny home for yourself or your family, there are quite a few things to consider. In general, tiny houses are meant for small families or couples. Some people have managed to make a tiny house work with two children, but you will have to consider this when you are either buying or building your tiny house.

Michael McCord

If you enjoy your knickknacks or are a collector that deeply enjoys surrounding yourself with your collection at all times, then this is also not for you. Also, if you have a hobby that requires a lot of storage space, you might want to take that into consideration. Tiny homes are meant to cover the essentials, but in a comfortable way. Imagine being able to walk into your home and being able to see your entire living space, if that appeals to you, then you are on the right track. However, if that thought is appalling and you could never imagine this in your future, it might not be for you.

A great way to think about this is take a walk through your home and take inventory of everything you have. Now think about everything you really use on a daily basis. Most people are surprised with the amount of things they own that they really don't use, or are just completely unaware of why they even still have it. On the other hand, people in tiny houses can give you a detailed rundown of not only their belongings, but how they play a role in their everyday lives, many of which multi-task.

I am not saying you must give up what you love in order to live in a tiny house, absolutely not. Moving to a tiny house just means that a cleaning up of your life might be necessary. If a hobby is crucial to your happiness, find a way to make it work for you, and maybe cut something else out. No two tiny house journeys are the same, and that is okay. You are going to find what works for you and your lifestyle and stick with it.

Many people say that one of the hardest part of building a tiny house, is well, building the tiny house. They lose the motivation to continue when they realize how much labor actually goes into their creation. One of the best ways to prevent this from happening is to make sure it is something that is incredibly important to you. If you are on the fence about it, you could just be wasting your time and money, and no one wants that.

Tiny houses are not a new concept; it is more of a throwback than a movement. Some people describe it as the return of the Sears house, back when they were cheap, small houses that were much more affordable than the larger homes the upper class were favoring at the time. It is too easy to forget that we generally have more than we need, including space and in some cases complete rooms.

Not everyone has a need for a large home and can even begin to feel burdened by it. It is easy to wake up one day and realize exactly how much time and money is spent on its maintenance. For some people, they make the decision to spend this time and money on other things. For those people, the first step they make is to simplify their lives. That is one of the reasons the tiny house movement is so popular, it gives people the chance to make things simpler for them. They do not have to worry about a high mortgage, or taxes. This will allow them the freedom to spend the money they saved on things they have always wanted to do.

If you have a larger family, you will probably want your home to be more stationary, so your children can go to school. There are communities of tiny houses for this exact reason, made for other people who also want the benefits of tiny house living without the desire to travel. On the other hand, some people choose a tiny house simply for the fact that they are mobile and they can take their homes with them wherever they decide to go. As you can see, there are many different options available to you.

You can choose to build your own tiny house, or purchase one already made, that is also your choice to make. Some people even decide to forego a restroom altogether and install an outhouse on their property or come up with other arrangements. These are just some of the things to think about when you are deciding which works best for you and your needs. Of course, there are standard designs for tiny houses, but with their increasing popularity different styles are now offered. You will learn about the different standard designs to see if you find that one that suits your specific needs.

Advantages of a Tiny House

Less clutter, part of living in a tiny house means that you will be unable to make purchases that you don't truly need. This is will lead to less unnecessary spent, especially for those people who depend on therapeutic shopping.

You will spend much less time cleaning. This is obviously because less space means less area that requires cleaning.

One of the biggest appeals for tiny house living is the overall savings, you will save money on all utilities, taxes, home improvements, and there will be no huge mortgage to pay.

Lower carbon footprint, tiny homes just use less. They produce less waste, use less energy, and consume less resources.

The tiny house revolution has a created community of like-minded individuals who are more than willing to help each other. Many people consider this to be one of the biggest appeals.

Disadvantages of a Tiny House

Organization is a must, one small pile of clothes or a small mess can take up a more space in a tiny home. So staying organized is very important if you want to be comfortable in such a small space.

Entertaining can be quite difficult, you can only fit so many people in a tiny home comfortably. So if dinner parties and large gatherings are a common part of your life, you might want to take this into consideration.

Storage, tiny houses to do not have long hallways and large closets to store those items you don't want the world to see. This is when creativity becomes important, but the good news is, hidden storage opportunities are everywhere, you will just need to do your research and find what works for you.

You can't take it all. This is one of the most difficult obstacles to overcome. When people begin taking stock of all the items they own, they realize their lives are full of family heirlooms, random objects, and things that just hold large amounts of sentimental value. Some people find these items too difficult to part with.

Each state has different codes and laws surrounding what constitutes a house or an RV. It can be confusing and frustrating trying to figure them out while still getting the house you want. Sometimes these two will just not meet up and a tiny house in the middle of hundreds of acres is just not a legal possibility. Make sure to look up and fully understand your regions specific codes so you are not breaking the law. Nothing would be worse than spending all that time and money building a tiny house, only to not be able to use it.

Now that you have a general idea of what it takes to live in a tiny house, it is up to you to decide if it is right for you. Statistically, 68 percent of tiny house owners do not have a mortgage compared to 29 percent of more traditional home owners. Also, 55 percent of tiny home owners have more savings in the bank than other homeowners. These savings add up quickly and are very enticing to groups who never thought they would have the money to ever own a home.

The initial costs for a tiny home are also much less than a traditional home. As a matter of fact, some people have managed to build their entire house for under 10,000 dollars, using second-hand materials and reconstituted items. The cost of heating and cooling a tiny house is a fraction of a larger home, giving you more money to spend on the things you have always wanted to do.

Chapter 2:
What is a Tiny House

A tiny house is exactly what it suggests, a much smaller house than what most of us are accustomed to. Tiny houses are not actually a new concept, it is just that throughout the decades our homes have just gotten bigger and bigger. We have all seen older houses that seem drastically smaller than the neighboring homes. The average tiny house is 186 square feet, but remember this is an average, so the sizes do vary. The average American home is 2,600 square feet, so you can see how much smaller this truly is.

There is also some slight controversy in the tiny house movement, because the term tiny is subjective. What one person might consider tiny another person might consider simply small. One couple live in a house that is 120 square feet while their friends live in a home that is 400 square feet. Some people might consider both to be tiny while others might think one is tiny and the other small. Some people think the line separating the two is whether or not it will fit on a trailer, which is usually the base for a tiny house. Others think that if it is within 700 square feet it is a tiny home. That being said, a tiny house or a small house, they are still out of the norm and can be environmentally friendly while still providing the necessities.

Tiny houses represent more than just a smaller living space. It is considered a movement for a reason after all. The idea behind a tiny house is cover all the basics for humans to survive, but just doing it in a way that does not consume so many resources. Tiny houses are made to be environmentally friendly and cheaper over all. Millennials have a tendency to be more inclined to consider a tiny house because they are the generation with the most student debt. Many do not find it feasible to enter the job market, pay a mortgage, and living expenses in order to live comfortably. However, they also do not want roommates or to move in with their parents, so tiny houses is a good option for them. The average cost for a tiny house is 23,000 dollars, which is much more affordable.

Comprehensive Beginner's Guide for Newbies

This image is a good example of what tiny house looks like, as you can see, it really is tiny. However, that doesn't mean you have to give up traditional comforts. There is generally a loft for a bedroom, a fully functioning restroom, kitchen, and living room area, all of which are just on a smaller scale. The tiny house community has a tendency to be a DIY community and people have come up with some very creative ways to make their tiny houses feel much bigger.

The whole idea of a tiny house movement is to live a bigger life instead of a having a bigger house. The essentials can easily be met within this space, what you choose to do with it after is completely up to you. By choosing to live in a tiny house you are making the decision to simplify your life and remove the unwanted clutter around you. Tiny houses are often built on trailers and can easily be moved. For some people that is the basis of their appeal.

For those just entering the job market, their futures are not set in stone and relocating is often a possibility. A tiny home reduces the stress of finding a new place to live, because your house can be brought with you. If that is the case, you would definitely want to construct or purchase your house on a trailer.

Because of the limited sizes of tiny houses, it is much more affordable to use top quality materials, that would otherwise be much too expensive in a larger home. So that fancy marble you've always wanted in your kitchen, but never thought you could afford because of the amount needed would no longer be an issue. Also, tiny houses are not one size fits all, there are numerous ways to alter them in order to meet your needs. Some people prefer to have a loft and an open design downstairs. Others choose to have smaller separate rooms, in a more traditional manner.

In addition to tiny houses there are also micro-houses and small houses, all of which are very similar in size. There is some crossover in the sizes of these three, but in general a tiny house or a micro-house is under 500 square feet. Some people would disagree, but just in case you are looking up information about tiny houses, it would help you to know that some floorplans might just be too large for what you had in mind when you thought of your tiny house.

The Logistics: Frequently Asked Questions

How do they get electricity? This is a bit of a complicated issue, because it depends on many different variables. First, you need to have a general idea of the amount of electricity you will be using and where you intend to park it. If you are parking in an RV lot there will be hookups for you to use. If you choose to live near someone you know that will allow you to run a heavy duty extension cord that will work as well.

One of the most popular ways is to use solar power, and there are kits that are sold for this exact purchase. Other people, who live far away from other people and in areas where solar power is not the most reasonable choice, they will call the power company and pay the necessary fees to have electricity run to their home. Keep in mind that this can take some time and can be expensive, but some people still prefer to do it this way.

Also, tiny houses can have traditional outlets for televisions and other household appliances. Later when you are working on your plans for you home, you will need to know where you put ach of the

Do they Have indoor plumbing? Plumbing is also a major concern for those constructing a tiny house. It is a simpler set-up similar to an RV or camper and can be done for pretty cheap. Some people also opt for composting toilets or container toilets. A lot of people also collect rain water to use as their water supply. This technique often requires a larger, separate apparatus in order to catch enough water for daily use. In addition, tanks of water are often needed to be brought in during dry months.

When choosing how you want your water supply the easiest option is a tank and pump, this will provide you will the running water that you are most accustomed too. However, this has its drawbacks, first off, they must be filled, either by bringing in jugs of water or by finding a hose. The larger the tank you choose means the longer it will last, but it also adds quite a bit of weight. Some people think it will also be an eyesore and take up a lot of space in a tiny home, but many people find creative hiding places for larger tanks such as under their sink. You can even have a hybrid of the two, by having a tank for when you are not near a camp that has hookups, but installing the necessary pipes and hookups that would allow you to connect to water source when it is available.

Getting water out of your tiny house is also a concern, for instance, there is more than one type of water. Grey water is water from your sink or washing machine that has not come into contact with feces, black water is water that has come into contact with feces. They must be disposed of in designated areas only and sometimes these locations are difficult to find. Grey water cannot be dumped into existing waters such as lakes or rives because it can pollute it, however it can be used for your own garden and in designated areas with plants since they have the natural ability to filter it and use it positively. Different areas have different laws about this, so make sure to read up on where it is safe to do this. Below is an image of a tank that is used to hold the grey or black water until there is appropriate place to dispose of it.

Comprehensive Beginner's Guide for Newbies

Black water on the other hand, has to be disposed of in appropriate locations. The easiest ways to this is to find a dumping station, many RV camps have these and many urban and rural locations do as well, you just have to do a little research to find these. There are weight restrictions involved with tiny houses so it is important to know the rules associated with your location and to dispose of both grey and black water appropriately and not exceed your weight limits.

If you know you are going to have a permanent location for your tiny house, then you can also simply connect to the regular sewer system that is available to you. Again, not everyone is going to have this option. People generally use a mixture of these options to find what works for them.

It is also possible to have internet too, usually in the form of satellite or cable, which can set up mostly everywhere, even in the most remote locations. Some people choose to purchase contract free hotspots since they travel so often, and just one of the many new options available to you.

Sewer issues can arise if you decide to have a more stationary home, but for a few hundred dollars a plumber can have you hooked up to a local city sewer. In order to be able to do this you must be up to codes. This will involve doing the necessary research that is specific to your state.

What about heating? There are also many different options when it comes to heating your tiny house. The first thing you need to consider is how powerful your heater needs to be, take into consider the weather and seasons of your location. Some people choose to use a wood burning stove as a heater, while others prefer a propane heater or fireplaces. Good options for either of these are the ones meant for houseboats or small cabins, since they are so compact and take up such little space. Gas in another popular option for heaters and many different companies

Comprehensive Beginner's Guide for Newbies

make some small enough for a tiny house's needs. The good thing about heating a tiny house, is that it usually only takes one.

Can I have a traditional stove? When it comes to cooking options, it is very similar to heating. You can purchase a wood burning stove, one that runs on propane, gas, or even alcohol. There are many different alternatives available to you when it comes to which fits into your lifestyle the best. You can also choose to have a full or half stove.

Many recommend looking into stoves meant for houseboats, cottages or RV's because of their size and ability to be used in small spaces. Others opt out of having a stove at all and prefer to keep a small grill with them in order to do cooking outdoors. Again, this is all up to what you want and what will suit your specific needs.

What about bathing? If you choose to have a bathroom in your home, you will need a way to bathe yourself, whether it be a shower, bath, or a combination of the two. Showers are a bit more common simply because they take up less space. The bathroom itself will be very small in general, and a small shower cubicle with a water conserving showerhead is a wonderful option. Some people like to use horse troughs at the bottom of their shower to reduce the amount of water escaping with a wrap-around shower curtain or sliding glass door to create their showering cubicle.

Comprehensive Beginner's Guide for Newbies

Others simply put a drain in the middle of the bathroom floor without a separate cubicle at all, just being making sure everything kept in there would be safe it wet. This seems strange to many of us, but can really go a long way for saving space.

There is always the option of a full bathtub, but that does need more water and more space. If having a bathtub is one of things that you require to live happily, it too can be done though. They work better for people who will not have to depend on a water tank, and are instead hooked up to a local water supply. Some people simply devote the majority of their bathroom space to the tub, while others have been a bit more creative and hide their tub underneath a movable table or bed. This is one of the many examples of how tiny houses can encourage creativity when utilizing the limited space.

This should give you a better understanding how a tiny house works and the many options that are available to you when choosing the path to your own tiny house. Remember, that everyone is different and what works for one person, might not work for you. It just so happens that one of the best parts of a tiny house it that you can make it what you want it to be, since they can be so easily altered.

It should also be noted that some people choose to forego somethings altogether simply because it fits into their lifestyle better. There are some who choose not to have a bathroom in their house at all, instead choosing to use public restrooms because they are traveling more often than they are not. Others just do not consider a kitchen a priority because they would rather eat out or cook outside. There is nothing wrong with this, it is just personal preference. Just remember, how you decide to have your house set up is completely up to you.

Chapter 3:
Wheels or No?

Now let's discuss your plans for your new home. There is still some red tape to go through in order to live in a tiny house, the laws haven't quite caught up yet. For instance, in some states they can be considered home-made RV's, but not all states have this distinction. If you purchase your tiny home outright then it is easier to get them certified as an RV because of the business from which you purchased it has the power to do this. For the average person building their tiny home, they do not have the business license in order to make this claim.

These issues could be referred to as the dirty little secret of the tiny house world. However, people have found many ways around these rather archaic laws. Traditionally a tiny house is built on a trailer, which makes it mobile, however, more and more people have decided that this particular type of tiny home does not suit their needs. This is especially true for couples with children. Now, there are some other options available to you, each coming with their own set of problems.

Which is Right for You?

- Do you have children and need to be in a more stable environment?

- Would you like to be part of a more solid community?

- Would you rather be hooked up to a sewer and water system?

- Do you plan on staying in one place for a long time?

- Are you stable in your career and feel as though frequent relocation is not an issue?

- Do you plan on travelling often enough that you would rather take your home with you?

- Does your job require you to travel to numerous locations for extended periods of time?

- Do you have access to an RV camp that functions year round?

- Is owning land important to you?

By asking yourself these questions it will be easier for you to decide which type of tiny house is more appropriate for you. Constructing your

Comprehensive Beginner's Guide for Newbies

tiny house on a trailer is no longer the only option, it is just the most common. Every state has different laws and codes that dictate what is and is not an RV and how long one can live in it. For the most part, they do not allow people to call it their primary home. However, not states are the same, so do your research and work with the system instead of against it. If you do decide to keep your home on a trailer, make sure to look up your state's specific codes and abide by them. If the laws prohibit you from living in an RV, having it certified as one could work against you in the long-run, so make sure you have a complete understanding of what you expect and how you can make it happen.

Trailers come in many different sizes and are all meant to be able to safely hold a certain amount of weight. You will need to have a weight estimate that includes everything you intend to have in your house. If your trailer is too small, this could lead to a dangerous situation, not to mention it can be a costly fix. It is safer to get a larger trailer and not meet its maximum weight limit than to expect too much from a smaller trailer. You will also need a vehicle capable of hauling your trailer as well, if you do not already have one, this is another crucial aspect. Other tiny house owners found themselves in this specific predicament and included this in their funds for their homes.

In addition to the trailer as the base of the home, there are two other options. One is to build your home on a solid concrete foundation similar to a traditional home. This is ideal for people who have no intention of traveling and want to stay in one place. The other is build your tiny house on a combination of pallets and concrete, this is considered to be more stable than a trailer, but still easily moveable if the situation calls for it, consider it basically a medium between a trailer and a foundation.

One of the most common loopholes is to rent land from someone who already has a house on the property because many states allow what is called ADU laws, or accessory dwelling unit. This would mean you would not own the land, but you would be able to make it more stationary and live in it year round. This is not for everyone, because they feel as though it is not permanent enough. However, do not simply overlook this option altogether because plans may change in the future. Many tiny home owners started off this way with a hybrid foundation that allowed them to easily pick up and transport their house to their more permanent location.

Comprehensive Beginner's Guide for Newbies

Many states and cities now have what is known as tiny house communities. They already have the necessary utility hookups available and people can either rent or purchase the land their house sits on. These are popping up everywhere, and some people pick out their tiny house community before they have even constructed their tiny house since it is the basis of the appeal for them. If you decide to take this route, the internet and word of mouth is a great way to find an existing tiny house community. More of them exist than what people think, mostly because they do have a tendency to be slightly hidden or slightly off the grid. Some of them are even self-sustaining, but that doesn't mean that they wouldn't welcome other like-minded people with open arms.

One of the most successful and newest trends is to consider cooperative purchasing. Many groups have started chipping in and buying land in a location they love specifically for starting their own tiny house community. Land is expensive, and all it takes is a few like-minded people to start a community of their very own. This has been done in many different states and cities with much success. Again, it is easy to break the law without knowing it, so make sure you contact the proper people to make sure your community is up to code and what you are doing is legal. It is easier to make the necessary changes as you go, than it is when everything is finished.

Some cities just simply allow tiny homes. They do not have a minimum requirement of square footage and as long as the basic necessities are met, there are no other laws to be dealt with. Each place is different so it is difficult to have a solid answer, other than, do your research and go to your local government agency to figure out how to make it work. Many tiny house owners say the best thing to do is to speak to a contractor who understands your goals, they will know how to explain the codes and permits needed to make your dream a reality.

Even if you own your own land and decide to live in a tiny house, your state might be one of those that has a minimum set for square footage. If this is the case, a tiny house just might not be a possibility as a main home. Speak to a contractor and have everything explained to you. If you find yourself in this position, you could build your home on a trailer and have it certified as a RV to use occasionally, or you might consider making a lifestyle change and moving. It all depends on your life's specific path and where you want to go.

Comprehensive Beginner's Guide for Newbies

Getting a copy of the International Code for one and Two Family Dwellings is a great place to start when it comes to a tiny house where children will also reside. Every state abides by this and it is updated frequently so make sure to get the newest version. Read about what you would need to do to ensure your tiny home will pass. In addition, the Recreational Vehicle Industry Association is a great resource as well. There are many different rules and codes to follow, but it is always more helpful to know what you are dealing with than not.

Many people wish this part was easier, and in the future as the popularity of tiny houses increases, it probably will be. However, as of right now, it is very much a learn as you go journey. Each state is unique and some are easier to navigate than others. However, the good news is that there are successful and happy tiny house owners in all of them. So even though it might seem difficult and discouraging in the beginning, it is possible.

Chapter 4: The Building

Alright, after you have decided which type is right for you, the trailer, pallet, or with a foundation, now it is time to build your tiny house. Obviously you will need quite a few building materials and how you decide to obtain them is up to you, new or used, it is your choice. Remember, tell the people in your life about your new project, it is human nature to want to help. Some people also have a habit of accumulating things and before you know it, you might have nearly everything you need simply from friends and family happily donating it to you. Craigslist and restores are perfect for finding cheaper materials, and with a little cleaning things can look brand new. Bartering is also a great way to get some of the materials as well, chances are, if you are going from a large home to a tiny house, you will have plenty of items that you no longer have a need for, these items will be great for bartering.

At this point in the process you should have done your research and figured out where you are going to put your tiny house and what style is right for you. The basic materials are all going to be the same regardless if you are using a trailer or a cement foundation, which is good because it makes things much easier. This is a beginner's guide and will give you a general idea of what you will need, depending on your own personal choices you will probably need to add to the list.

Let's Begin

Either in your current home or outside, tape off a section the size you want your future tiny house to be. You need to see exactly how much space you will have and where you plan on putting your things.

Visit other people with tiny houses or even tiny house hotels to get an idea of what you want.

Begin going through your things, be honest with yourself about what you truly want and need. You can make room for the things that are most important to you. The same goes for things that really aren't that important, if you don't wear it or it doesn't serve a purpose, don't keep it.

Learn to curb your shopping habits. This is challenging for many people because it is so engrained to American culture that many people don't realize how often they shop and how much they depend on it. Remember, you just won't have the necessary space.

Your Location

- Spend time where you plan to put your tiny house. Some people choose to build a small garage or a deck, look around and find the best spots for these if they are something you have been interested in.

- If you are building your house on a trailer, make sure you have a list and understand all the necessary codes and laws that you will need to make it a certified RV.

- If you are going to park it at a camp visit, find some potential spots and figure out the water and sewage hookups you will need.

- Locate the correct place to dispose of the grey and black water, this is very important, so make sure you not only understand where, but how to do this.

- For a stationary home, go ahead and make the plans to set up your plumbing, sewage, and electricity needs. These are going to be the areas where professionals are important, so take advantage of their skills and know-how. Do not be afraid to ask questions, this will make your journey that much easier.

- Determine your budget. Just like any house, this will take money, but how you get your materials will have a lot to do with it.

- Also, most of us work, and tiny houses do not happen overnight. If you plan on building it yourself, make a rough draft of a schedule that will make it easier for time management.

- Be honest with yourself about you are capable of, somethings should be done by a professional. If you are not a certified electrician or 100 percent sure you know what you are doing, hire someone who does. Not only do you want to be safe, but you need it up to code, the same goes for plumbing.

- Decide how you want to attack your building strategy, do you want spend some time gathering your supplies a little at a time? Or would you rather save up enough money to get it all at once?

Choose Your Floor Plan:

- You are going to want to find the plans for your home. Pick one that suits your needs.

Comprehensive Beginner's Guide for Newbies

- There are many premade designs to choose from, but you can always make your own if you want.

- Depending on the size of your house and the design you choose, your material list will change, so make sure your plans are thorough.

- Know the exact measurements of everything you will need. This will save you some time down the road and minimize scrap.

- If you choose to purchase your design plan, it will more than likely come with a list of materials that you will need. This is a great starting off point for someone who has little to no experience building.

These are different examples of common floor plans for tiny houses that are on a trailer. Typical tiny houses on trailers are no more than 13'6" high and 8'6" wide, the size variation comes from the length of the trailer and the style of roof. Again, these are just basic examples, there are many different types and styles out there. Even if you choose to purchase a floorplan it can be altered to suit your needs. You can make big changes or smaller changes depending on what you need and want in your tiny house.

Michael McCord

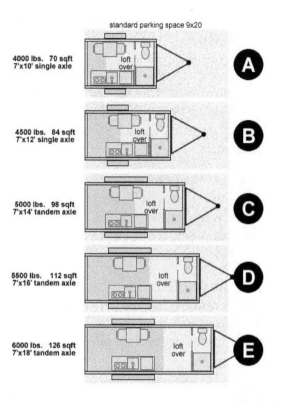

This is an example of a stationary floor plan. In general these can be made to be a bit larger and their shape can vary more than the confines of the trailer base. Some people though, depending on the laws and codes of an area, some people will build right up to the legal limit that makes it legally habitable year round. In the end, this may seem like less of a tiny house and more of a small house, however you decide to build your tiny home is up to you.

Comprehensive Beginner's Guide for Newbies

  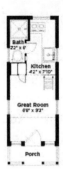

Roof Types:

Not all roofs are made the same, some are easier to construct than others. Some make snow removal easier, while others are better for more moderate climates. Choose your roof based on a combination of your level of skill as well as your location.

Shed Roof – This is a great option if you want to build a loft and utilize space. It is a one-side roof that allows you to have the peak of your roof at the maximum height of the structure. You can also add windows on the peak side giving you additional lighting. The pitch will dictate how much space you have on the eave side of the structure.

If you plan on collecting rain water this style of roof is also perfect for that since it needs to be collected on only one side, making it easier for you. If you live in an area where it snows quite a bit, you will need a higher pitch to make sure the snow falls off. When considering materials for your roof, snow falls off metal easily.

Saltbox Roof – This is a good option if you want a two-sided roof, but with the added space that comes with the shed roof. The saltbox roof is very similar to the shed roof, but its peak is just off-center to one side of the house. The advantage is the added space and that it is aesthetically pleasing, but this style will not work in all environments.

There are many disadvantages to this style of roof, for instance the off-center peak needs to have the end walls fortified under the peak. This means you shouldn't have a window or a door on the main floor under the peak, but instead to the side of the long roof. The off-center peak causes it to be structurally weaker than other roofs. This type of roof also means that load weight from either rain or snow will be greater on one side of the peak. This can be compensated with additional reinforcements, but that means more material and it will take up more space.

Gable Roof – This is the most common type of roof, it is a simple two-sided, center-peaked roof. It is also the easiest to build, but it does waste the most space. A loft in a gable roof has little storage space and just enough room for you to crawl into bed. However, if that is all you think you will need this is perfect, it also doesn't take much to learn to properly cut your roof trusses and secure them while building. Keep in mind though, this is the second weakest roof, the saltbox being first. It doesn't take much to reinforce it for strength, but doing this will take up to a foot of headroom away from your already small loft. If you are in an area where it snows often, definitely reinforce it though because without it, the roof couldn't hold the weight.

Barn Style or Gambrel Roof – This is a good choice if you want a center peak and a larger loft area. This style of roof offers you added height and width in the loft area and is more structurally sound than a gable roof. This type of roof is also the most difficult to construct because it is a total of 8 angled cuts for each roof truss which also needs to be reinforced at each joint for added strength. This type of roof also requires the most roofing material.

Flat Roof – Many people just say, don't do it. They are incredibly susceptible to the highest damage when it comes to the elements. There is no pitch so they have the most leaks and require the most repair. If you live in an area where it snows often, imagine all the weight of the snow just sitting there with nowhere to go. That could be a recipe for disaster.

Appropriate for the Climate:

When you are constructing your new home take common weather patterns and the harshness of the seasons into consideration. It is estimated that around 40 percent of household energy is used for temperature control. So, when constructing your new home plan ahead for both the colder and warmer months. If you take precautions early, you will save yourself time and money later.

Climate Tips:

- If your house is on a trailer, the floor can be very cold, so make sure to also insulate the floor. This is often forgotten, but it can go a long way in keeping your feet warm and a more pleasant winter.

- Choose your heating source based on your climate, a propane stove made for a boat might work for a more moderate climate, but would not be enough during a harsh winter. For areas such as the northern states consider investing in propane direct vent wall heaters.

Comprehensive Beginner's Guide for Newbies

- Invest in mobile home skirting and wrap pipes in coil heat tape, then glass insulation wrap, followed by a plastic overwrap to keep pipes from freezing. Once this is finished, encase all of it in a larger pipe leaving a little bit of dead space.

Now that you have a better understanding of your options when it comes to your tiny house, you should be more confident in making the right decisions. Use good judgment when deciding what is important to you when purchasing materials, if you live somewhere where the winters are harsh, try your best to insulate the entire house. This will save you money in the long run and make you more comfortable.

Chapter 5:
What to Expect

At this point you probably already know which style of tiny home you want, either stationary or on a trailer. You have probably looked at dozens of potential floor plans or even began making one of your own. Maybe you have even began gathering materials and watching tutorials. You already know that building a tiny house can take a while and that you must dedicate some time to it. One of the best ways to speed up the process is to stay organized.

After you have chosen or created your floor plan there are some general things that will make your construction run smoothly. If there are things you don't know how to do, ask some friends, people will generally jump at the chance to help you. Even if you have provided some sort of incentive, dinner or a little cash goes a long way. In order to keep costs low, rent the tools you don't already own or can't borrow.

The following list will give you a general idea of everything that you should have lined up. If you purchase a plan these things should be, but might not be included, and if you made the design yourself, take the time to include everything.

Master List:

- Cover sheet, this is a rendering or a detailed picture of how the house will look when built. Make sure it contains all sides, even an aerial view.

- A foundation plan, if you are not building on a trailer, this should include the exact dimensions and show where the walls, pads, posts, beams, footings, bearing walls, and retaining walls will be.

- The layout or floor plan should have the exact dimensions indicating the layout of the rooms, windows, doors, ceiling heights, and plumbing fixture locations. These plans show the layout from an overhead view.

- Roof plan, this is exactly what it sounds like, it should include a detailed plan for the roof you choose. It should include the materials you choose to use as well as the ridges, valleys, and hips in the roof.

- You will also need an exterior elevation, this is a 2d representation of the front, left, right, and rear sides of the house.

Comprehensive Beginner's Guide for Newbies

Measurements, details, and materials should also be included.

- Cross section or wall section, this is basically a cut-away view of the house that show where one thing is in reference to another. This is when important changes in ceiling or roof heights are noted, and different levels are shown in relationship to one another. This will also show the exterior details such as railings, bandings, insulation, and flooring or roofing details.

- You will also need a detailed electrical plan, it will need to show where lighting fixtures, outlets, and switches will be.

- This is a tricky one, because as you build, you will find that you might be adding to it quite frequently, but it is good to have a general idea. This is a bill of materials, or a list of all the materials you need to construct your tiny house, this will include everything, trailer, cement, lumber, doors, windows, hardware, insulation, and so on.

- If you purchased your plan, you will probably also have a complete step by step set of building instructions for your particular design of tiny house. If you do not have this, set aside some time and write out your own set of ideas about when and where you should start and what you will need for each project. Some people like to schedule out exactly what they hope to accomplish each day so they can keep making progress.

Chapter 6: Common Mistakes

Despite the wealth of information out there about tiny houses and tiny house living, mistakes and errors will still be made. Obviously, the best thing to do is learn from other people's mistakes and avoid making them yourself. The tiny house movement is predominantly a DIY community and people are more than happy to share what they've learned, more often than not, through trial and error. Throughout your journey and construction you might find yourself sharing what you've learned too.

Common Mistakes:

Trailer Size – One of the most common mistakes people make when picking out their trailer is not taking into account its load capacity. Trailers are built with axles connecting the wheels which are meant for certain load capacities. Each axle is capable of carrying a certain amount of weight, this is called the Gross Weight Vehicle Rating. For instance, a double axel trailer where each axle is rated for 3,500 pounds means that the total weight is 7,000 pounds, which also includes the weight of the trailer itself. This means that you will need to have an accurate estimate of how much your tiny home will weigh once all the furnishings and materials are included, plus the weight of the actual trailer itself.

Vents – Make sure to include vents in your roof, this will prevent the growth and spread of mold. No one wants to spend the time and money to replace a ceiling. It seems simple, but can often be forgotten.

Hot Water Heater – Many people have made this mistake, the internet is full of horror stories of what can happen if you put an outdoor water heater directly in the bathroom. This can release carbon dioxide or generate too much heat. You can either purchase a different type of hot water heater or you can build a small shed outside for it. Either way, if it is meant to be kept outside, do not ignore this warning.

Windows – Your first instinct might be to purchase windows that are the same size as the rough openings, they won't fit. This could turn out to be an expensive mistake. Look at the windows before you purchase them, they generally have a sticker on them that will say the rough opening dimensions they will fit. Also, aluminum windows will be cheaper, but they are not very good insulators. Even though they are a

Comprehensive Beginner's Guide for Newbies

cheaper alternative, you will regret it during the first harsh winter.

Siding – If your house is built on a trailer keep in mind that it will be moving, fast. Work with aerodynamics in mind, because if you don't you could end up losing panels and siding on the road. Also consider rain or even hail when driving. You will want to make sure your windows are made of a very strong material and are 100 percent leak proof. This is definitely something worth spending some extra time and effort on.

Codes – This really cannot be stressed enough, each state has different codes and laws in reference to houses. Make sure you are up to date on all of them and make wise decisions. There are many horror stories of people not doing their research and being unable to live in the houses they spent so much time building.

Hopefully some of these mistakes will help you during your construction. Just remember that it is easier to do a little at a time, one of the most common mistakes people make is underestimating how much work and labor actually goes into constructing a tiny house. Set realistic expectations and pace yourself. If you need help don't be afraid to ask for it and if you need to hire a professional, do so. Your goal is to live big in a tiny house, it will be difficult to do that if you are forced to do constant repairs.

Helpful Hints:

- Try playing around with the plans you have for your house. Build a life-size replica from cardboard to get an idea of what you would like to tweak. You can even go as far as making sinks, a couch, counter, and so on out of cardboard too, so you know exactly what it will look like.

- Think of one thing that you simply cannot live without, something that makes you happy. Make sure you have room for it in your house. This can be anything from an easel and paints to an espresso maker. Whatever it is, if it is important to you, then it deserves to be in the house too. This may sound obvious, but when you are faced with having to go through everything you own, you will start to see exactly how much just simply won't fit in a tiny house. For some people this can serve as a rude awakening, but it helps if you already have an idea of what is truly important.

- Learn the difference between a want and a need. This sounds simple enough, but a significant part of our lives involves chasing after things we want after our needs are met. That is part of what a tiny house does, it allows you to separate these things by only letting you be surrounded by what you need. Retraining yourself to live simply is no easy task, but it can be incredibly rewarding.

- Make sure you have windows, you do not want to make it feel as though you live in a shoe box. By definition a tiny house is well, tiny, but it doesn't have to feel claustrophobic. So when you are designing your house imagine where you would like the windows to be and why. When you make the life-size cardboard version take it outdoors, add some windows, play around until you find where you like them best. The natural light will make the small space feel larger and much more open.

- Find other tiny houses and make friends with the owners. There are open houses in many cities throughout the United States, this will give you a chance to see a tiny house in all its glory. You might even make some friends along the way.

- Make a checklist of everything you can think of in reference to your tiny house. Not only will this help you stay organized, but it is incredibly gratifying checking things off as you progress.

- Organize a friend help day. Cook some food, make some drinks, play some music and invite all your friends over to help you with the things you are unable to do alone. This will make it fun while also being helpful. This can also help to boost your morale and make the process less stressful. One of the biggest challenges to a tiny house is staying motivated long enough to finish it. Life has a tendency of getting in the way and never giving us a break which makes it too easy to slack off on the things we don't immediately need.

This list should help you organize your thoughts and set up a general plan of action. Add to it slowly if you need to, everyone has to start somewhere and there is nothing wrong with taking your time. You are making a big decision, so take it seriously and make sure you feel comfortable with each and every step of the process.

Chapter 7: Interior Design

This chapter will be about how to maximize the space you have and making your life as comfortable as possible. For instance, walk around your house and look at all the objects that you use which serve only one purpose. There are so many different ways to create items that can multitask.

Creative Storage:

First, furniture such as a bed or a couch can also be used as storage. You can build a bed frame that has drawers or is able to be lifted so clothes and linens can be kept underneath. If done properly, the bed will not look any different than a bed you would find in a traditional house.

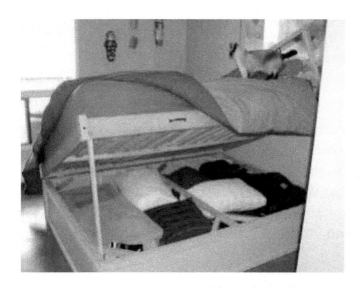

You can do the same to the couch, all the space underneath the cushions. You simply need to reinforce the top and you can either use basket storage underneath or make it so each section can be lifted.

You can also use your walls for storage, the space between wall studs is the perfect place to add thin, built-in cabinets, imagine a medicine chest. Half-wall dividers, like the ones typically used between a toilet and a vanity are perfect for a tall roll-out shelf. If your home is already built and you decide to add these storage options be careful not to cut unto any electrical wires, do it safely.

Comprehensive Beginner's Guide for Newbies

If you bought your cabinets, they often include one of the faux drawers. We all know the one, it looks like a drawer, but serves no real purpose. This is a simple solution, turn it into a real drawer, it doesn't have to be full sized, even a small drawer can hold spices or utensils.

Cabinet door interiors are a perfect example of wasted space, stock up on strong self-adhesive hooks for things such as measuring cups, spoons, tools, brushes, and other items.

Boxes, crates, and barrels, if it holds things you can mount it on the wall to make chic and affordable shelves. Too much of these will only add clutter, so use this technique sparingly.

Magnetic strips are another creative way to store knives, paperclips, tweezers, etc. However, if you intend for it to hold heavier objects it will need to be reinforced, the adhesive alone will not be able to support the added weight. Magnetic strips are also cheap and can be hidden on the backs of cabinets.

The tops of doors are often overlooked as potential locations for shelves. Since they are higher up, put objects that are not frequently used on these shelves, simply for convenience reasons. This can also work on the tops of windows too; spices or jars look great above a kitchen window.

For storage that is out of sight, stairs are a perfect place, each step can be built to be lifted to create additional storage space. If your tiny house design has built in stairs leading to a loft, this is prime storage space. You can also paint each stair a different color, to add a pop of color and to help keep you organized. Other people will only see the different colors; however, you will know the colors are your personal way of staying neat.

Comprehensive Beginner's Guide for Newbies

Strategic Decorating:

Another option that creates much more floor space is fold-down furniture. This is most commonly used for tables and desks, but with some creativity and imagination you can come up with other fold-down furniture ideas. Some people have made entire fold-down benches to make extra seating. When it is not in use, it just looks like the wall, so you are also not sacrificing style.

Shelves, shelves, and more shelves. Build the shelves into the walls instead of bringing them in after. You can place shelves nearly anywhere in the house and they can be used for everything from toiletries to pots and pans. In addition to shelves, use your wall space efficiently, such as hanging utensils in the kitchen. This will also free up some cabinet space too.

Keep things clear above the waist, with the exception of the kitchen. Doing this makes the house feel more open and prevents you from bumping into things with your arms which can add to stress and the feeling of being closed in.

Light colors make spaces seem larger, so if your first instinct is to paint your walls a deep shade of blue, you might want to rethink your color choice. Opt for lighter shades, and if you still want a bolder color, pick an accent wall.

Comprehensive Beginner's Guide for Newbies

Invest in some mirrors. Strategically placed mirrors also open up a small space. Some tiny house owners made an entire wall a mirror, but that is not necessary for everyone. Just make sure you have at least one mirror that is tall enough to show your entire body, this will open up your home and give the illusion of more space. Mirrors reflect light, so if you feel as though your house could use some more natural light, hang a mirror opposite a window where the sun will reflect the most sunlight.

Avoid having unnecessary walls and partitions in your home. If you have an open floor plan, your house will appear larger. Partitions and walls will separate a small space into even smaller spaces, this is not what you want. If having separate rooms is important to you, make sure you take that into consideration during the designing of your floorplan. Some people fix this issue by having two lofts, one on each side of the house. This would require a larger trailer or foundation, but if having this space is important to you, there are ways to make it work.

If you insist on having walls, consider purchasing sliding or collapsible walls. They will provide privacy when needed, but will not always be there to make the space feel smaller. If you want a more affordable option, curtains are also an easy alternative.

If your house is stationary or you intend to leave it in one place for an extended period of time, you could do what many others do and build a deck. Some people choose to make this a larger addition, often with more open space than their actual homes. They use this space as a place for yoga, entertaining, or any other activities that they do not have room for inside their home. Others decide to have a more modestly sized deck to match the size of their home. The deck does not need to be attached to the house, so it can be easy to separate the two if you find yourself in a position where you need to relocate in a hurry.

The Purge:

As you can see, there is only so much you can bring into a tiny house. When people decide to downgrade they go through what many people call "the purge," which is when they sell or donate all the things they are not going to bring with them. Many people take this time to learn about themselves and consider it to be a cathartic experience. Doing this can be very overwhelming and is often much more emotional than people assumed it would be.

If you and a significant other are doing this together, depend on each other to make good decisions. Some people suggest making initial toss and keep piles. Then go through the keep pile again and talk about the reasons you want to keep it. Try to reduce the keep pile until it is a realistic amount. You made the cardboard house for a reason, put the things you want to keep inside it if it helps you get a better idea of how much stuff you can realistically fit. Many people find this helpful.

Many people explained that when it came time to go through their belongings, they gave back. If you want to make some extra money have a yard sale or even donate everything to a local second hand store. One tiny house blogger wrote that she put everything she couldn't take with her in her front yard and had a free sale. She said that it felt good knowing that she was giving back, since she herself got so many of the materials she needed for her the construction of her tiny house from people who were just giving it away.

Learning to adapt to a tiny house can be very challenging, but one of the best ways to acclimate is to celebrate the things you do have, instead of the things you want. Never lose sight of why you wanted to move to a tiny house to begin with. Your reasons are your own, but it helps to remind yourself of these reasons when you begin to feel overwhelmed. Tiny house regret is fairly common, especially in the beginning, it is a different lifestyle altogether. So don't be too hard on yourself if you have an emotional reaction. That is only natural.

Chapter 8: Success Stories

There are many success stories of people who live happily in their new tiny homes. Some of these people acclimated quickly to their new homes, while others had a rockier road to success. Either way, there are many people out there who are living big in their very own tiny homes. In fact, many of the best stories are not just single people, but entire families who are making a tiny house work for them. So even if your transition starts off rough, just think about how difficult it had to be for others until they found their own rhythm. If they can do it, so can you.

One inspiring story is that of a special needs teacher named Jessica Bolt from a poor area in North Dakota. She chose not to build her tiny home because of the demands with her job, and purchased it from a company in Minnesota. It is 196 square feet and boasts amenities such as a washer and dryer and an incinerating toilet that burns its contents to ash. Her decision to purchase the home was due to the fact that she wanted to be a home owner, but thought the cost for an average sized house was out of the question. So she did some research and chose to purchase a tiny home on a trailer.

When she was researching what type of tiny home she wanted, she paid the most attention to finding a company that was already located in the north, she thought that a company in California just wouldn't understand what negative 40 felt like during the winter. She chose hardwood floors because that is what she grew up with and made sure her house is roadworthy. She is very proud to say that she will never have to pack up a U-Haul again for this reason. She chose to pay off the company in a series of payments that are less than what she was paying in rent for her apartment and in a couple of years, it will be paid off and she will be the homeowner she has always wanted to be. Her tiny house was a dream come true for her and she had no issues at all adjusting to the size. The stairs leading up to her loft are all hidden storage and she is in the process of hooking up to local electrical and water lines. She has only had her tiny home for two weeks, but already couldn't imagine going back.

Another story of a family in Oregon gathered some attention because a family of four downsized to tiny house that is only 317 square feet, including the two separate loft areas, one of which is split in two for the children. They decided to make the switch because of the high cost of utilities and general living. They chose to build their tiny house themselves on the same property as their 1,000 square foot home. The married couple was also in the middle of a major job change by starting their own construction business.

They chose to build their tiny home on the lake they loved so much and decided that it would be a good idea to home school the children. So not only would they live in a tiny house, but they would spend quite a bit of time in it. Their experiences varied from stressful to enjoyable, for instance trying to help their children adjust to the much smaller space. They admit that this style of living might not be for everyone, but it has helped them come closer as a family and to leave the consumer-driven society they wanted to escape from. She says their tiny house journey is still continuing and learning, and hates to be connected to the term 'tiny house movement,' because she thinks this sounds like a fad. She insists this is more of a throwback than a trend, and they are simply getting back to the way things were meant to be.

Michael McCord

Architect Macy Miller spent decades living in the real world, but after graduating with a Master's degree she decided she wanted a fresh start. That is when she started to consider a tiny house. It was during this time that she met her husband and soon after welcomed their first child. She did not let this deter her, and she made her tiny house design based on how they lived their lives.

She and her husband built their home themselves, and during the construction she became pregnant with their second child. She quickly altered the plans and made the necessary adjustments, with the house being 232 square feet. She made enough room for her toddler and a nursery area for the new arrival. She admits that it was not an easy journey, but now could not imagine living any other way. They have saved more money than she thought possible at this point in her life and truly enjoys the way they live.

As you can see, not all journeys are the same and it is possible to change your plans to make them more appropriate for your specific needs. Everyone faces their specific set of obstacles, but with a little determination and creativity it is possible to get the exact house you have been looking for.

Comprehensive Beginner's Guide for Newbies

One of the best success stories when it comes to tiny houses is rather famous among the tiny house communities. Wesley Birch and his wife purchased a plan for a tiny house in 2015 and began construction immediately after. They only used second hand materials and did all the work themselves. In the end they had a 24-foot-long tiny home complete with a full bathroom, full size gas range, large pantry, mid-size refrigerator, double basin sink, and plenty of storage space, all for under 8,000 dollars.

If there was something they did not know how to do, they watched tutorials and read how-to's until they were confident enough to do it themselves. They did not even have a truck to pull their tiny house in the beginning, and had to purchase one to get the job done, which he paid 1,300 dollars for. He checked the free section on Craigslist multiple times throughout the day and was relentless is in his pursuit of cheap or free materials

Not only do they love their new tiny house, but they did it in a way that was even more cost efficient than an already cheaper alternative. This is has led many others to challenge themselves when it comes to what they are capable of, in both terms of building and being frugal.

There are many different reasons to become a member of the tiny house movement. No matter what your personal reasons are, this book will help you get on your way to living a more simple life. A community that depends so much on trial and error and a DIY mentality is unique and can be very enlightening.

Comprehensive Beginner's Guide for Newbies

You know what your options are now and how to get started. Now it is up to you to choose when and how to do it. Just remember to be honest with yourself about your intentions and reasons for making this life changing decision. Take your time when choosing a design, and if cost is an issue for you, be patient and take advantage of all the different websites and people around you that are willing to help. Learn from other people's mistakes so you make less of your own and if you do, fix them and move on. You know what to pay attention to, such as the climate you will be living in and which roof will work the best based on this.

If you decide to purchase a floor plan, make sure it fits into your lifestyle and if you need to make small changes to it, do so. This is your tiny house, and you are not only allowed, but encouraged to make it adapt to your life. Have fun and enjoy the journey of the creation of your new house. You are well on your way to living big in a tiny house.

Conclusion

Thank you again for purchasing this book!

I hope this book was able to help you to decide if a tiny house is right for you.

The next step is to pick a floor plan, location, and start gathering your materials.

Finally, please consider checking out our Amazon Author page at https://www.amazon.com/-/e/B01LYIFPLO.
Here you will find numerous books describing all you need to know about Rental Property Investing, Flipping Houses, Real Estate Investing, Real Estate Sales, REITs, Credit Score Repair, and more on Tiny House Living! If you check out our Real Estate Library, you are guaranteed to profit from Real Estate Investing and turn this into a lucrative income stream for the rest of your life. Don't miss out!!

Last but certainly not least, if you found this book useful in anyway, a review on Amazon is always appreciated! You can write a review on our book's page which can be accessed through this link:

Michael McCord

https://www.amazon.com/Tiny-House-Comprehensive-Beginners-Construction-ebook/dp/B01LZS2Y7Q/

Thank You and Best of Luck!!

Tiny House Living

Cardinal Rules for Ditching Your Clutter and Your Mortgage

Michael McCord

Copyright 2016- Michael McCord - All rights reserved.

This document is geared towards providing exact and reliable information in regards to the topic and issue covered. The publication is sold with the idea that the publisher is not required to render accounting, officially permitted, or otherwise, qualified services. If advice is necessary, legal or professional, a practiced individual in the profession should be ordered.

- From a Declaration of Principles which was accepted and approved equally by a Committee of the American Bar Association and a Committee of Publishers and Associations.

In no way is it legal to reproduce, duplicate, or transmit any part of this document in either electronic means or in printed format. Recording of this publication is strictly prohibited and any storage of this document is not allowed unless with written permission from the publisher. All rights reserved.

The information provided herein is stated to be truthful and consistent, in that any liability, in terms of inattention or otherwise, by any usage or abuse of any policies, processes, or directions contained within is the solitary and utter responsibility of the recipient reader. Under no circumstances will any legal responsibility or blame be held against the publisher for any reparation, damages, or monetary loss due to the information herein, either directly or indirectly.

Respective authors own all copyrights not held by the publisher.

Introduction

Tiny house living is desired by many, but only a few pull it off for life. What seems wonderful during the planning and building stage can quickly turn against you, when you are living the "dream."

It seems magnificent when you are watching shows like "Tiny House Nation" and "Tiny House Living." People describe all the benefits, a few of the hiccups during building, and changes they had to make after living in their tiny house for a few months. But, the reality is often much different than what is shown on television.

Do you think a family of six is really still living in 100 square feet? No, when circumstances become better and life returns to affording a mortgaging for a full size home, you can guarantee the tiny house is up for sale.

If you do a search for tiny houses to buy, you will see quite a few, throughout the USA for sale. Often the captions read, "like new, lived in, but need to sell." In other words, for whatever reason going tiny didn't work for the owner. Several tiny homes have been converted to rentals because the owners no longer want to live in such small structures.

Michael McCord

The question becomes—how can you be a part of the tiny house movement that is successful? How are you going to be the one that makes it work after spending $10,000 to $100,000 on your tiny house creation? It is by following some of the cardinal rules that make tiny house living a reasonable choice.

You have a lot to consider before you build your house if you want to become successful. The success factor comes in when you consider having no mortgage and decluttering your life to fit the "small" style you have chosen.

Learn how you can make your tiny house living arrangements successful from planning all the way through to living the "dream."

Chapter 1: Downsizing within Reason

The greatest benefit of going tiny is gaining a mortgage free life. But, there are challenges to keeping your life free of any mortgage payment. The first challenge is "going tiny." Yes, it is a benefit, but it is also a challenge because you have to learn to live in a space that may be a quarter, a half, or three-quarters of the home size you are used to. There are certain rules that will make the choice to downsize easier.

The Right Size

Numerous studies have been conducted by experts on how much space the average American needs to feel comfortable in their home. These experts state that 100 sq. feet per person is the smallest amount of space the average person can live in. If you have four people in your family, you need at least 400 square feet for your home. Ideally, 500 square feet is better, so you have 100 sq. feet of community space.

Every person, no matter how close a family they are, needs time to themselves. It is not reasonable to expect that the great outdoors will always be able to provide you the space you need away from others. Freezing cold temperatures, where frostbite happens in seconds, if you go outside can hinder your "space." Temperatures in the 90s to 100s, or higher can lead to heat stroke. Thunderstorms with lightning, hurricanes, or tornadoes can also prevent you from going outside. Yes, these storms do not last, but what if you are cooped up for 3 days? Can you survive if you only have 10 sq. feet per person?

Most people find that sometimes there is such a thing as too tiny. The right size is all about knowing yourself first, and then knowing the other people you are going to live with, in your tiny home. If you are a married couple, with no plans for children in the next five years, then you may feel comfortable with only 200 sq. feet. But, what happens if birth control did not do its job, and you have a baby before you planned? Can you live in 200 sq. feet with a baby or for those five years before you can afford a larger home for your growing family?

The situations mentioned and questions asked do not mean you are going to answer the same way as the next person that reads this book. Rather, you are thinking about the "what ifs" and determining who you are as a person.

Cardinal Rules for Ditching Your Clutter and Your Mortgage

For example, one person interested in building a tiny house is comfortable living in a small amount of space, without anyone else living in that same space. However, this person knows that there is a need for high ceilings. An eight-foot-high ceiling is not enough, despite being just over 5 feet, eight feet high ceilings makes this person feel closed in. If there is not at least 4 to 5 feet of floor space running from the front to the back of the tiny house, without walls, the person also feels closed in. If you know things like this about yourself, then you can either plan to build a home that fits your quirks or you can immediately know that tiny house living is not for you.

Vehicle and Trailer Costs

The discussion on size must include the two options you have for building your tiny house: trailer or fixed home. A trailer can affect your downsizing benefits. Have you watched some of the tiny home shows on TV? Several people have built their home for $10,000 or $20,000 on trailers, but was the show specific? Did the show state the cost to build the house was $10,000 and this included the trailer? Most are ambiguous on this point. Typically, the shows are all about how much the materials, furniture, and labor costs were for building the house, but don't actually include the cost of the vehicle or trailer you need for towing your tiny house.

The next cardinal rule for reducing your monetary constraints is knowing what the vehicle and trailer will cost you in addition to the building materials.

Each vehicle and trailer has a GVWR or gross vehicle weight rating. It can also be called the GVM or gross vehicle mass. This is the safe operating weight/mass your vehicle can have. It includes the vehicle chassis, body, engine, engine fluids, fuel, accessories, driver, cargo, and passengers. For the trailers, it includes the chassis, axles, floor of the trailer, and all other trailer components.

Let's say you have a truck that says it has 6,200 pound GVWR, and the vehicle weighs 5,000 pounds. What do you think you can safely carry inside the vehicle? If you said 1,200 pounds, then you are correct. If you add a 300-pound tongue weight trailer, then the amount decreases to 900 pounds for the vehicle. So, including passengers and what you carry in the actual vehicle, you can carry 900 pounds, with a trailer.

Cardinal Rules for Ditching Your Clutter and Your Mortgage

The truck has to be able to tow the trailer size you want to have based on towing capacity and GVWR. Most ¾ ton or 1 ton trucks can pull the maximum trailer size for tiny homes.

Most states allow you to have up to 60 feet with a truck/trailer length. You may be able to drive an RV that is towing a vehicle and be up to 65 feet in length. For a trailer and motor home situation, which is the closest to a tiny house set up, you can be up to 45 feet in length, with a maximum height of 13 feet 6 inches.

Now, you understand the background information. It is time to discuss the costs. For a brand new 1-ton truck with a hemi and heavy duty rating, which is required for pulling the largest tiny house size, you would need to spend anywhere from $50,000 to $75,000 for the vehicle. If you are willing to fix up a used vehicle, you may be able to find an HD hemi 1-ton truck for $25,000 to $40,000.

Certain online tiny house retailers sell trailers for a maximum of $7,000, which is their 26-foot trailer. Other places may require up to $10,000 for a trailer that is set up for tiny house creations. You can also spend as little as $1,000 for a trailer, where you may need to spend a little more adding axles and welding the bolts to the trailer to secure the frame of your tiny house.

Let's say you are going for the larger tiny house, thus you need at least $50,000 for the newer vehicle and $7,000 for the 26-foot trailer. Already, you have spent $57,000 for the tiny house, without factoring in the building costs. Will this get you away from a mortgage or loan?

You might need an auto loan to fund your traveling tiny house, which may not bring you any further ahead financially. Remember that most auto loans are paid off in 5 years or less, thus your monthly car payment can be extremely large.

Now, if you already have a vehicle that can tow the trailer or already bought a trailer, these costs could ensure you get away from borrowing money from a bank. Everyone's situation is different. It is just a consideration you have to make when determining if you can stick with the cardinal rule of not having any type of loan at all to create your tiny house.

Land Costs

The thought that a tiny house is more affordable when it is not fixed to a piece of land can be somewhat of a myth depending on where you want to live. Obviously, some individuals want the mobility of a tiny house, but if you have no intentions of traveling then you may be better off finding a land deal.

Although rare, there are still some states in the USA that offer cheap land. It may not be in the most glamorous of locations, but if you work from home like many traveling tiny home owners—it may not matter where you live.

The downside is if you want to live in the city, such as New York, New Orleans, or other big cities, you may be right back to paying a mortgage for 200 sq. feet. Some tiny homes have sold for $250,000 to be in downtown New York, Charleston, or New Orleans.

There is one rule of owning land that can be appealing to tiny home owners. Land accrues equity, rather than depreciating like a vehicle and trailer. Land when it has a home on it, has more value. If you spend $50,000 on a piece of land and $10,000 to build your home, then you have at least $60,000 in value. The key, of course, is being able to find the right situation.

Land can also help you reduce current mortgage costs. You may not be entirely mortgage free for 10 years, but you would have a lower mortgage than if you purchased land with 2,000 square foot new construction built on it.

If you want to downsize to avoid high mortgages or any mortgage at all, then you will need to be savvy in your exploration for land. You could also approach friends or family that own land. You may be able to get 1 acre to build your home on for a reasonable value, if you know someone with land to spare.

An important rule is to go with what is most affordable as a means of avoiding the mortgage you ordinarily need for a home.

Avoid Expensive Tastes

Tiny houses do not have to be expensive, but they can certainly be unaffordable. One family built a tiny vacation home for $125,000. The home was around 200 square feet. This family wanted only the best in construction and technology. They wanted a tiny smart home, with

Cardinal Rules for Ditching Your Clutter and Your Mortgage

a long granite countertop, wireless technology, and much more.

Your expensive tastes will increase the bill. This next rule asks you to think about what is most important to you, so you can avoid the mortgage or loan most homeowners end up with. It is also about making sure you do not blow the budget you have and spend more of your savings than you allot for the project.

If you want a full size fridge because you do not want to visit the store every two or three days, what are you willing to sacrifice in order to afford the appliance? When it comes to your bathroom vanity are you willing to spend $500 or can you make do with buying material for $60 and building your own vanity? To keep costs low and yourself mortgage free, you must be willing to compromise and sacrifice certain things you may desire.

Downsizing Steps

1. Determine your comfort level.

2. Examine your true self for space needs.

3. Do you need a land to accommodate your space requirements?

4. What is your budget?

5. Once steps 1 through 4 have answers, you may begin designing and planning for your tiny house.

Chapter 2: The Building Materials

Keeping with the discussion of being mortgage free, and your tastes, we must discuss building materials in more detail. You are working out whether you can truly live tiny, not only in the affordability sector, but in other ways. Once you figure out how much space you need to live comfortably, whether land or a vehicle is more affordable or feasible, and that you must sacrifice some things you love, you are ready to determine how much your tastes really cost.

Granite vs. Butcher Block

Run a search on a lumber company website like Home Depot. How much is a piece of butcher block that is 8 feet (long) x 2 feet (width)? One store sells a block countertop that is 25 inches (wide) by 8 feet (long) x 1.5 inches (thick) for $159.00. If you search that same store, a piece of similar pre-fabricated granite countertop in white is $199.00. If you shop in stores that HGTV uses for their shows, then you should consider a granite countertop to be $50 to $100 per square foot. It also depends on the thickness of the granite and quality. The building materials you use determines whether or not you are spending $10,000 on building your home or ten times that amount.

Free vs. Paid

Many of the homes you see on TV had special supplies. People took the time to hunt around and find free barn wood that they restored and used to keep material costs low. Are you capable of doing the same? Do you have the time to spend hunting bargains, helping someone take down their barn for the free wood, or tearing apart pallets for the wood? It also has a lot to do with experience.

You may not have the experience to build without a contractor present. If that is the case, then you may not be able to save on the building materials as much as an experienced laborer who has access to free materials.

It would be nice if you can build your home for $10,000, but remember it all comes down to your tastes. Are you willing to sacrifice certain things like time, appliances, or granite countertops to be mortgage free? If you are, then you may be able to find many of the materials you need to build the house at a lower cost, ensuring that you won't need a mortgage to build your home.

Weight Determines Materials

Not only is the cost going to determine whether or not you have a mortgage, but the weight will play a part in certain choices you can make. This applies only as a rule to individuals who are going with a truck and trailer setup. You have to be cognizant of the gross vehicle weight rating for your truck and trailer. If you go for a granite countertop in your kitchen, the weight will be more than butcher block. One is wood and the other is rock, so it does matter. Your rule is to ensure the weight of your tiny house is within the appropriate maximum.

The benefit of this rule is that you will have to be less extravagant of decluttering your belongings further to account for the elegance of your tiny house on a trailer. The size and weight of belongings, such as clothing, books, computers, and other personal items you bring into the completed home, will determine the weight of the building materials.

Yes, when not moving, the gross vehicle weight rating is less important, on the other hand, if you have ten people in your home, with an axle that is already loaded to capacity with just yourself, then you are going to have issues.

Not having a mortgage is one extremely powerful benefit of going tiny, but if you want to survive tiny, then you also have to make allowances for the weight and thus the overall design of your tiny house. People do not succeed in going tiny, when they forget some of the very basic rules of building.

Engineers and architects are brought in on building projects because they have the expertise to ensure a structure is safe based on longevity and weather. A home in Colorado has to make allowances for heavy snow and ice weighing the roof down versus a home in North Carolina that needs to withstand hurricane winds.

You might save money on building materials, but can they truly get you down the road? Will your reclaimed barn wood withstand hurricane strength winds, when you are doing 70 miles an hour on the highway?

Cardinal Rules for Ditching Your Clutter and Your Mortgage

Going mortgage free is great, unless you sink money into a project that will be completely wasted after one trip on the highway.

It sounds negative. It makes going tiny seem really unappealing right now.

You should be asking yourself—is there a silver lining to the discussion?

Yes, remember the discussion about "knowing yourself," before you start your tiny house dream? The silver lining is based on your own perception.

Are you willing or capable of reducing your monthly expenses in order to get the tiny house of your dreams? You cannot be willing to sacrifice quality of building materials and overall construction because it will create safety concerns. However, when you follow the building material rules and suggestions, you can make a safe home, for a decent price, to avoid the mortgage you don't want to have anymore.

Building Material Steps

1. Determine the appliances, type of woods, countertops, and other building materials you like best.

2. Visit a lumber company or other location to price materials.

3. Once you have a list of things you want in your tiny home, speak with an engineer.

4. Have the engineer determine the weight of the materials based on their professional knowledge.

5. Modify your building material list based on cost and weight.

Chapter 3: Off the Grid

You have a choice when you build a tiny house on a trailer. You can choose to be off the grid, unsupported by internet, TV, energy companies, and other utility companies. Living off the grid allows you to get away from the conventions of the world and live a simpler life. For some individuals this is a great option. For others, they like to be energy efficient, with certain creature comforts. There are ways you can make tiny house living more comfortable for you, while reducing certain amounts of clutter. It is going to depend on the amount of money you wish to use to build your tiny home. The motto is to keep away from mortgages and loans, which could limit your desire to build a more energy efficient home that is semi or completely off grid.

Solar Power

Your home size will determine the number of solar panels you will need to live off grid. For a solar power system, you require solar panels, a controller, battery, and inverter. The battery is going to accept the charge from the sun, while the inverter will convert the battery energy into usable electricity in the home. Good batteries for a solar array can run upwards of $400 or you can purchase batteries like those for a car, but you are going to replace those more often. You can purchase solar panel kits that offer 400 watts for under $1500. Other systems offer more wattage based on the number of panels and can run upwards of $20,000 depending on the system and the panels you purchase. Of course, there are definite savings after the fact.

First, you will not need to find a location that supplies you with an electrical hookup. Boondocking becomes more of an option, when you don't have to consider finding a power source.

If you are not mobile, then you do not have to sign up and pay for any energy company to supply you with electricity. You save because you are no longer paying out a high monthly bill or any bill at all.

The initial cost may be higher, but the overall savings and lower carbon footprint make solar power the best option for tiny houses.

To figure out the number of solar panels you need, you have to know the draw of your electrical devices. Do not forget any electrical

Cardinal Rules for Ditching Your Clutter and Your Mortgage

device you might be using, if only sometimes plugged in. It will all matter.

Here are common devices you might have:

- Laptop
- Tablet
- Smartphone
- Fridge/freezer
- Washer/dryer
- Stove
- Coffee maker
- Toaster
- Mixer
- Light fixtures
- TV
- Hair dryer
- Curling iron

Anything you plug in is going to draw on the solar energy. How much it draws depends on how long it is plugged in, whether it needs to run like a fridge to keep cool, or if you can use the battery for a few days before you need to plug in the device again. Obviously, the fewer items you keep plugged in throughout the day, the less you are going to draw on your energy.

Propane

Propane also needs to be figured, when designing your tiny house. A propane tank will take some weight consideration, as well as how much you need to carry before you need to get a refill. If you are using any propane hot water heater, or gas appliances, then you may need more than a regular sized tank. You might need two propane tanks. Another thing to consider, in order to make your tiny living successful, is how easy will it be to switch out the propane tank or tanks? If you are in the middle of the desert for three weeks, where civilization is 100 miles away will you have enough propane?

It is the little things that can make traveling more difficult in a tiny home. When space is at a minimum and you don't have basic necessities, it is possible for tempers to flare. One way to avoid this and be happy in your tiny house living is to plan correctly for the situations you are going to be in.

Water Tank

Water is a similar discussion to propane. You need to know you have enough clean water for the basic necessities, but also be cognizant of the weight. For water tanks, you have a clean tank and a gray water tank. Anytime you shower, wash your hands, or wash dishes, you are going to have gray water (dirty water). This water has to be disposed of at proper locations because of the soap and other chemicals that are in the water. You have to plan to have enough water on board to avoid running out when you need it most. A 400-gallon water tank is not small and it is very heavy when filled with water. A family of four may require such a tank, with a fill up every other day. One person may be able to drive around with 200 gallons in their water tank for a week before needing to fill up the water tank. It depends on the number of showers, cooking, and other uses you have for water. The rule is to think about it, determine the size of tank needed, and factor this into your plan as a means of determining whether you should declutter other aspects of your life to fit an important need—water.

Other Utilities

In a day and age where computers, tablets, and smartphones are everything in our existence, you may feel you want to be on the grid just a little for certain utilities such as TV and internet. But, is it possible with a mobile tiny house? Can you find a cost effective way to stay hooked into the media?

The short answer is yes, but the longer answer is that it all depends on you. What do you use your internet for? How often do you watch TV? Are you more likely to stream an entire season or do you have to watch the show when it first airs? If you work and travel, then how often are you on your computer using data?

For example, if you stream internet TV for 4 hours a day, spend 8 hours surfing the net doing research, and sending 100s of emails a dongle from Verizon or any other mobile phone service provider is not going to provide sufficient data for your internet needs. Companies like Comcast and Century Link are land based.

Cardinal Rules for Ditching Your Clutter and Your Mortgage

This leaves you with satellite internet and TV. A lot has occurred in five years, where you can now find better satellite internet packages, although they are more expensive than land based companies. It does give you the option of staying hooked in to the online world. TV is as simple as choosing which satellite provider you like best and then directing the satellite in the right direction based on where you have stopped for the time being.

Off the Grid Steps

1. Ascertain if solar power is within your budget.

2. Use online websites to determine the draw of your appliances.

3. Use the information from step 2 to buy the solar panel package required.

4. Determine what appliances use propane.

5. Assess how much propane is required for standard operation.

6. Buy the needed tanks.

7. Calculating the weight of water.

8. Purchase clean water tanks and gray water tanks based on the weight of water.

9. Request price quotes from utility companies for TV and internet, if you wish to be semi-off the grid.

Chapter 4:
Parking your Tiny House

Another challenge you will face is where to park your tiny house. Your goal is to be mortgage free, with less clutter in your home. However, what is going to happen when you need a place to park your mobile tiny house? Will you be able to find a location? Will your tiny house be welcome? Unfortunately, there are more and more restrictions each year, when it comes to parking your tiny house in certain locations.

Tiny House Communities

Certain cities around the USA are starting tiny house communities. Lyons, Colorado and Portland, Oregon are two places that have tiny house communities. Some RV parks in California have allowed tiny house constructions.

Your challenge is to ask whether some of these communities are safe. Are they a place you would want to raise children? Like RV parks and manufactured home communities, you are going to have all varieties of people living in the area. You will want to do your due diligence to ensure you are choosing a safe place to park, while traveling.

Not all communities are going to be "free" parking. You may discover that the fees are just as high as RV parks. Rental fees will be discussed later on in more detail.

RV Park

In the last year or two, RV parks have been changing their mind as to whether you can park your tiny house. As with many mainstream communities, people living in RV parks are deciding that tiny houses are not uniform to RVs and are too individual or too oversized to be in an RV park. Perhaps, it is more that RV parks are hard to come by that are affordable and RV travelers do not want their spaces taken up. Unless you ask at each location, the reason you may be turned away will remain unclear. It is known that RV parks are certainly getting stricter. It makes it difficult to find locations to park, outside of land friends and family may allow you to occupy when you are in the vicinity.

Boondocking

Boondocking is an RV term, used to describe staying on someone else's land or finding "free" land. Public land that does not require a fee for a camping location, but permits camping, is a great way to travel. Unfortunately, in the USA there are few boondocking locations available. The locations that are available are usually privately held, but provided to you for trade or a small fee. There are boondocking forums and websites, where you can locate places to stay.

Rent

Public locations that offer campsites, RV sites, or parking for tiny houses usually have site rental fees. These fees can be as much as a mortgage. Some locations charge more than $700 for you to park for a month.

It does not put you any further ahead to pay a high fee for spot rental, for a month, if you are paying the same amount for the site rental as you would for a mortgage on a $150,000 valued house.

Again, it does seem negative, when you read this information. But, do not get discouraged. There are certain people and communities, making tiny house living possible. The challenge is doing your research and finding locations to park, based on your travel desires. You have to go into tiny house living with your eyes open. The cardinal rule for this chapter is that you cannot assume you will always be able to find a place to park. RVs can usually get away with parking in truck stops or certain retail store parking lots, but a tiny house is more noticeable. You have to seek permission for parking when the land is owned by another. Just keep in mind that your research is paramount to making tiny house living a success based on your travel patterns.

Parking your Tiny House Steps

1. Plan your current trip.

2. Purchase subscriptions to AAA, boondocking websites, and RV parks.

3. Search for tiny house communities along the route.

4. Assess the possible locations for parking on your trip route.

5. Call ahead for availability and booking requirements.

6. Set up parking options along the route before you leave on your trip.

Chapter 5:
Decluttering and Guilt

Part of successful tiny house living is based on the functionality of your home. So far the discussion has been in how to reduce the need for a mortgage or how to live without spending a great deal on your tiny house life. Now, you will want to focus on the comfort of your home. The items you are able to bring into your tiny home are based on space, weight, and functionality.

A person with a stationary tiny home does not have to worry about weight, but you will need to be concerned with space and functionality. There are innovative organization methods, but "know yourself." Are you the type of person who will put away things after you have used them or do you let things pile up? Are you truly a person who can make your bed every day, when the necessity is there or will you avoid such a chore?

Living in a tiny house requires a hyper-organized and a proactive nature. If you cannot keep your space clean now, how likely will you be able to do so if you bring in a lot of things?

Michael McCord

There are definitely rules you must follow to declutter your life for going tiny, as well as to ensure you do not feel guilty when you get rid of something.

Decluttering Rules

1. If you have not used the item within the last six months, it goes.

2. Any duplicates of books, photos, or other items, you keep one.

3. Take photos of nostalgic keepsakes, then donate or sell them.

4. If you don't like it, and it was a present, it goes.

5. Find a home for all items or design your house to have a place for all items.

6. Start putting things away now, before your tiny house is built. Practice keeps you in an appropriate routine.

7. Think "someone else needs this more than I do." It helps you eliminate things you no longer use, and cannot take with you into your tiny home.

Cardinal Rules for Ditching Your Clutter and Your Mortgage

8. If you wouldn't buy the item today, it goes. If an item no longer fits into your décor, home size, or preferences, do not keep it.

9. Examine your spending habits. Do you truly need something that will add to your tiny house clutter?

10. Follow the rules and keep repeating them until you can eliminate all but the essential items.

Getting Rid of the Guilt Rules

1. Do you truly like an item you own that someone gave you?

2. Is the heirloom something you treasure because you find it attractive?

3. Have you ever given a gift that wasn't right, and wished the person would donate it or return it to the store?

If you have an item that someone gave you and you like it, keep it, if it is something you can fit into your tiny house. If the gift is unlikable because it is not your style or you find it ugly, remember, "It is your life!" Sometimes gift giving goes wrong. You cannot let the guilt weigh you down.

A coworker brought back soap from their month long trip. The person who received the gift is allergic to perfume. Should that person suffer the allergic reaction, and keep the soap? No. Should they feel guilty about giving it to someone else or getting rid of it? Of course, not. They also shouldn't make the gift giver feel guilty by not accepting the gift and giving a solid reason as to why.

You have honest justifications for getting rid of gifts others have given you, for taking pictures of heirlooms or passing them on to other family, as well as understanding that you too have given wrong gifts.

As long as you can accept the truth that not all things can be liked or enjoyed, you can donate, sell or trash items you do not need, want, or cannot fit into your tiny home lifestyle.

Chapter 6: Organizing Mistakes and Corrections

One of the most difficult parts of living tiny is having enough organization and space for the items you wish to bring. Many tiny house owners have added storage or removed built in options in order to gain more organization and storage. It is costly to remove things after you have built them, not only money wise, but also time wise. You purchased the materials, drew up the plans, and then you have to go in and modify everything. There are ways you can avoid these costly mistakes by following certain rules.

Tape off the House Design

Michael McCord

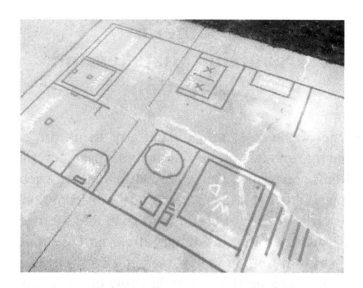

1. You will need to visit an architect to draw up house plans for you, unless you are capable of designing the house.

2. From the plans, tape or draw out the layout with proper measurements, either outside or inside your current home.

3. Include all areas you will have for storage.

4. Begin by bringing in the items that are most important.

5. Place these items in your design in the areas of storage you have.

6. Since the layout is not 3-D, you are going to have to use a tape measure to ensure

Cardinal Rules for Ditching Your Clutter and Your Mortgage

you are not stacking your items too high for the storage space you have. For example, in floor storage in a loft, is only as high as the joists you are using between the ceiling and the floor.

By laying out the design and testing the area with the items you have, you will know whether or not you have enough storage for the organization you wish to have in your home. It also helps you understand just how small tiny can be. You may end up changing the plan to fit your needs.

Bear in mind you also have vertical space.

You can use the walls for some storage, but not for everything. As you layout your design, think about what you can put on the walls.

Michael McCord

Clothing Issues

Clothing is one of the biggest issues tiny house owners have. How can they bring along the clothing they need for work, dinner parties, and other events? For some clothing is less important. One person may be happy with one outfit for every occasion, as long as they have five days of work outfits or uniforms. There have been other individuals that required a full walk in closet, which was possible based on innovative designs by professionals. Your clothing issue can be all about innovative concepts, such as how to hang your numerous scarves.

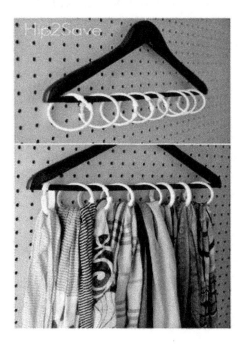

Cardinal Rules for Ditching Your Clutter and Your Mortgage

You can use shower curtain rings to hang scarfs on a single hanger. Another person used a circular tie rack to accomplish the same thing. The key will be to test the appropriate closet space for the items you own, as well as to look around at different locations.

1. Visit places like Ikea, which are known for their tiny room setups with closet space.

2. Take time to go to closet stores to see what they offer in terms of design.

3. Speak with a designer.

    You can always visit stores and speak with designers for free. You can take the ideas you see or are given and implement them into your tiny house.

4. Lay out your closet space, either in the closet you have now or by using tape to simulate the closet.

5. How functional is the space?

6. Can you fit everything you need?

If you can answer positively to steps 5 and 6, then you know the closet is going to work for you in your tiny house. If it is not functional and you cannot include all your clothing and shoe needs, go back to the drawing board.

Additions

Yes, additions or changes to your home are more expensive than getting it right the first time. However, there are some things that no matter how much time you give to plan for them that do not turn out as you hoped. Some tiny house owners have had to do the following:

1. Live in the house for a month.

2. Keep everything how it was the day they moved in.

3. Make changes after a month by adding more storage, removing certain furniture pieces, or building in others.

There are ways to avoid this issue. As you read in the other two organization sections, you can lay out your tiny house and test how functional it will be before you move in. There is no guarantee that it will work, but it is certainly an option.

Cardinal Rules for Ditching Your Clutter and Your Mortgage

Another step is to conduct research before you leave the planning stage.

1. Visit online storage sites.

2. Search Pinterest for storage ideas.

3. Go to tiny house forums.

4. Go to storage forums.

The more information you have, the easier it will be to create a tiny house that will work for you. Sometimes an internet search cannot be avoided. It is common sense, but you also have to know how to search.

Are you going to get ideas simply by typing in storage? Probably not. The keywords you use will help direct you towards the answers.

For instance, "tiny house storage hacks" brings up 1000 ideas on Pinterest. You will see ways to make extra storage, but not all of these ideas are going to be the correct option.

Case and point: storage between the studs.

Michael McCord

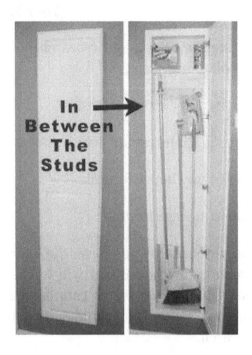

There is a flaw in this concept if you do not create the storage space correctly. This person bought a cabinet to prevent issues with insulation. When you leave a wall open, you have no insulation in that wall space. It can lead to inefficiency with your heating system. With a cabinet you are at least plugging any potential air leaks by using trim. Also between the cabinet and the studs, you still use a thin layer of insulation. If you just build shelves in the space, without proper insulation, then you are losing heat in winter or allowing hot air in during the warmer months.

Cardinal Rules for Ditching Your Clutter and Your Mortgage

Innovations exist and you may have a mind to come up with ideas all on your own. Just make certain you are not breaking the cardinal rule of this chapter: **test out the organizing ideas in a comparable space before you build it in a tiny house**.

Chapter 7:
Testing the Tiny

During the planning stage you are going to test the tiny house concept in all manner of ways. In recent chapters, the focus was on laying out the tiny house space with tape. In this chapter, you are going to find other steps to testing out the tiny for the success of living in your tiny house.

Rent a Tiny House

Remember the mention that some people are selling their tiny homes because they could not make it a success. Others who are no longer living in their tiny homes are renting them out. There is a whole online community where you can search for tiny house rentals from 96 sq. feet up to 1,000 sq. feet. You have the option of testing whether or not you could live in a tiny house with another person or your entire family.

It is imperative that you do so.

1. Search online for tiny house rentals.

2. Find a comparable tiny house based on the square footage design you are contemplating.

3. Rent the home for at least a week, but a month would be better.

4. Stay in the house with only the essentials.

5. Get a feel for how you need to adapt your life to fit in a tiny space.

At the end of the test, you may need to go back to your plan and modify it for more space, extra storage, or other changes.

Block Out Similar Space in Your Home

If you are unable to rent a tiny house due to the expense, then use the place you currently live in. This is where the tape will come in handy again.

1. Layout only enough space in each area of your home that you will have in your tiny house.

2. For the bathroom, tape off the sink, toilet, and shower area based on the square footage that will be inside your tiny home.

3. Do the same for each room, ensuring that you are not going over the "line" of space.

4. Rearrange the space you have taped off, so that what you need is within the lines.

5. Live this way, for two months.

Did you survive the test? Did you go over the line? Have you gone back to your tiny house plan to change certain parameters to make it easier to live in a tiny space? It is okay to answer yes, you had to modify your plan.

It is better to know that you are able to live tiny in the space you have because you have made a success of it already.

Conduct Tests with your Partner

For these tests, you do not need to tape off everything, but you do have to see how it will be to live tiny. It is not only about the space you will have, but the communication.

1. Start with the kitchen.

2. Set up an area of space that is comparable to the tiny house you are planning.

3. With your partner make a meal only in that space.

4. Again, bring only what you will have in the tiny house in that space.

5. See how you move with each other.

Did someone fall out of the space? Did you elbow your partner in the face, ribs, or step on their toes? Did you find you need to communicate better?

When you live in a tiny house, communication is key. While you are testing the tiny as the cardinal rule of planning, remember that open, voiced communication is the cardinal rule of living tiny.

If you have problems communicating now because you think the other person is just going to know what you want, then you need to work on your communication.

1. Start by being more vocal.

2. Do not assume the other person knows what you need or want.

3. Count to ten when you feel anger and try to communicate again.

4. Slow down. Your pace in life needs to be slower when you live tiny, to ensure you are thinking, listening, and communicating correctly.

Cardinal Rules for Ditching Your Clutter and Your Mortgage

5. Seek a communication class if you find you are still having issues.

Conclusion

Living tiny requires changes within yourself. If there is one cardinal rule you take away from this book—it should be that you need to know yourself better.

Until you can sit in front of another and tell them who you are, what your strengths and weaknesses are, and be open about your personality, without worry of criticism, going tiny will be difficult.

It comes down to being honest with yourself about what you can and cannot stand. If you don't know your weaknesses or do not like criticism, then when you live in a tiny house with another person, you won't have the open communication you need for your life to be successful.

All the rules in the world about how to downsize, use proper building materials, go off grid, parking your tiny house, decluttering, organizing, and testing the tiny will not work if you do not know who you are, your limits, and gain better communication.

Tiny House Living

Essential Strategies for Seasoned Tiny House Dwellers

Michael McCord-

Copyright 2017- Michael McCord - All rights reserved.

The follow Book is reproduced below with the goal of providing information that is as accurate and reliable as possible. Regardless, purchasing this eBook can be seen as consent to the fact that both the publisher and the author of this book are in no way experts on the topics discussed within and that any recommendations or suggestions that are made herein are for entertainment purposes only. Professionals should be consulted as needed prior to undertaking any of the action endorsed herein.

This declaration is deemed fair and valid by both the American Bar Association and the Committee of Publishers Association and is legally binding throughout the United States.

Furthermore, the transmission, duplication or reproduction of any of the following work including specific information will be considered an illegal act irrespective of if it is done electronically or in print. This extends to creating a secondary or tertiary copy of the work or a recorded copy and is only allowed with express written consent from the Publisher. All additional right reserved.

The information in the following pages is broadly considered to be a truthful and accurate account of facts and as such any inattention, use or misuse of the information in question by the reader will render any resulting actions solely under their purview. There are no scenarios in which the publisher or the original author of this work can be in any fashion deemed liable for any hardship or damages that may befall them after undertaking information described herein.

Additionally, the information in the following pages is intended only for informational purposes and should thus be thought of as universal. As befitting its nature, it is presented without assurance regarding its prolonged validity or interim quality. Trademarks that are mentioned are done without written consent and can in no way be considered an endorsement from the trademark holder.

Introduction

I want to thank you and congratulate you for purchasing Tiny House Living: Essential Strategies for a Seasoned Tiny House Dweller. This book is an intermediate level book geared towards the individual who wants to better educated themselves in the nuances of tiny house living. Detailed discussion covering the financial aspects of tiny houses, from how to afford your tiny home should you choose to build one yourself, to small details that could cost you thousands are included. Zoning considerations, construction and building guidelines are invaluable pieces of the puzzle. Rather than learn the hard way, we are here to help you. Ways to maximize your tiny space are important topics that are included as well. Tiny House Living is not just a trend, but a lifestyle. Our readers will learn the ins-and-outs, and the ups-and-downs of what to expect that many do not even consider when choosing to embark on this way of life.

Additionally, the art of Tiny House Living feeds into Real Estate Investing. We have many books on that subject that you can find by visiting our Amazon author page:

Michael McCord

https://www.amazon.com/-/e/B01LYIFPLO.

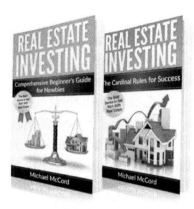

https://www.amazon.com/Real-Estate-Investing-Comprehensive-Beginners-ebook/dp/B01MQ0VTIU

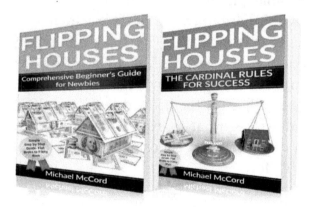

https://www.amazon.com/Flipping-Houses-Comprehensive-Beginners-Properties-ebook/dp/B01MQCR3OP

Essential Strategies for Seasoned Tiny House Dwellers

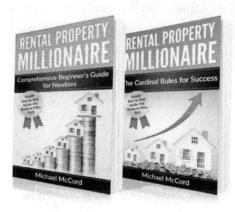

https://www.amazon.com/Rental-Property-Investing-Comprehensive-Investment-ebook/dp/B01M69Y22J

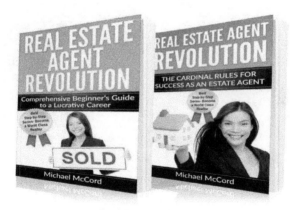

https://www.amazon.com/Real-Estate-Agent-Comprehensive-Generating-ebook/dp/B01M72UKYO

Michael McCord

But right now, let's explore strategies to maximizing your tiny dwelling and its benefits, and how to minimize mistakes and pitfalls of things you may not have considered when you were still new to the Tiny House lifestyle!

Chapter 1: Floor Plans & Design

Tiny Houses on Wheels

Deciding whether to design your own floor plans or buying a floor plan from another individual is an important decision to make. Depending on where you live, many considerations need to be taken into account before embarking on the adventure of tiny house construction. If you decide to draw up and design your own THOW floor plans, be certain that the following issues have been addressed:

- Do the dimensions of the floor plans fall within the guidelines allowed to be able to tow my THOW down the road or highways without a special permit?
- How much will my THOW weigh?
- Will the trailer be able to bear the weight of my THOW, and will my towing vehicle be able to tow the load safely?

Most states have a tow size and weight limit. If you want to build a THOW and be able to legally move it, dimensions must be taken into consideration and followed. Throughout the United States and most major highways, the size of your THOW may not be larger than a semi truck's trailer. Those dimensions are 13.5 ft. tall x 8.5 Ft. wide, and the length ranges from 40-60 feet long. Be aware, the height limits measure from the bottom of the tires of the trailer to the highest point of the roof of your THOW, so any roof fixtures such as stove pipes may need to be disassembled during travel. Ensuring that you do not cost yourself an arm and leg in tickets as you travel is important, as you aren't really saving money if you are paying fines and fees every time you relocate or move your home.

Another consideration is whether your trailer can handle the weight of your tiny home. To ensure a safe and sturdy home, your home should be built with construction grade materials. A 19 ft. long tiny home can weigh upwards of six thousand pounds without any possessions inside, and the longer your home is, the more it will obviously weigh. You aren't going to be able to hitch and tow six to thirty thousand pounds of home with a small car, so when considering your floor plans and design, think about the big picture. In most regions, a total weight (trailer included) of 10,000 pounds or less is ideal, as any further weight may require a special hauling license through the local Department of Motor Vehicle's office.

Essential Strategies for Seasoned Tiny House Dwellers

Other factors to consider when deciding whether to design your own home or buy floor plans from a professional is overall cost. There are many free and cheap tiny house floor plans for sale on the internet, there are books full of options, and a growing number of tiny house architects and manufacturers that will sell floor plans to you for a cost. The determining factor when deciding to buy or do it yourself is how much can you afford to lose? If you have no construction experience or are not able to read blue-prints yourself, design mistakes are an inevitability. Some mistakes will be easily fixed, while others can be extremely costly and take large, unexpected chunks out of your budget. Depending on your budget, your experience with construction and design, and how handy you are, it may be even cheaper for you to buy a pre-fabricated tiny home. A few ideas to help guide you if you make the decision to build your own design are:

- Consult with an architect, construction company, or structural engineer to go over your floor plans, and to check for any flaws or major issues of the design in question.

- Determine if you may need to subcontract certain design aspects, such as electrical and plumbing, to be certain building guidelines are met.

- If you choose to buy floor plans or hire someone to design your tiny house, do they guarantee your satisfaction or provide a warranty on their work? Are they accredited and licensed to provide the work being requested?

Keep in mind, consultation with any individual expert, licensed professional, or company will more than likely result in the expenditure of additional funds. Not many people will be willing to offer their services for free, unless you are fortunate enough to know an expert personally!

Tiny Houses on Foundations

Tiny homes that are not mobile and that are on a permanent foundation in a fixed location have entirely different standards of building and construction guidelines, but zoning laws still vary a great deal regardless of whether your home is mobile or not. With fixed tiny homes, design is more about what is desired by the soon-to-be occupants, what the minimum and maximum building codes for the region dictate, and meeting those codes and regulations. Design options are sometimes more fluid and plenty of variations of specific design and floor plans are easier to account for with fixed homes. Floor plans and design really come down to these things:

- Is your tiny house on a permanent foundation, or on wheels and mobile?

- What design aspects does your lifestyle dictate? What is necessary and what is needed in your home?

- How much space do you or your family need to live comfortably?

- Are you capable of building your own design, or will you need professional help?

- How detail oriented are you, and have you thought of everything?

As you can see, aesthetics is only the beginning when considering your floor plans and design options. Once you determine whether you want to live in a tiny house on wheels, or a tiny home that is in a fixed location, then determining what you need and want becomes a matter of what works best for your lifestyle.

Chapter 2: Financial Considerations of Tiny House Living

Financing Your Tiny Home

- How much does it cost to build or buy the tiny home of your dreams?

- Will the bank allow you to take out a loan to build or purchase your home?

- Can you afford to completely change your lifestyle and become a tiny home dweller?

The costs involved depend upon many variable factors. The first and most important is whether you are purchasing a tiny home that is already in existence (either stationary or on wheels), building your home yourself, or hiring a company to build a home for you. The real estate market for both stationary and wheeled homes is a new market that is seeing a big upswing in recent years, as many people see the appeal in spending more to live, those that want a simple retirement lifestyle, or the increasing amount of the population that wishes to become eco-friendlier and decrease their carbon footprint.

Pre-existing home prices range anywhere from around 4,000 for a basic 165 square foot home on wheels, to hundreds of thousands of dollars for high-end stationary homes located on ideal or prime real estate property locations. Many new tiny home manufacturers are springing up, offering an array of floor plan designs and prices range from roughly around $25,000 and up, depending of course on what the client's budget is and how many features are included. Most of these companies follow international building codes and can make modifications to existing designs per the customer's requests and needs.

If you decide to build your own tiny house, prepare to finance the build yourself, as traditional banks that offer mortgage loans do not offer loans for the buying or construction of alternative housing. There are a couple of options for financing, but they are not traditional and rates and fees are different for both. One way to possibly finance your tiny home is through a personal loan. Depending upon your credit history, credit score, and whether the lending company you choose agrees to it, an unsecured personal loan may be an option. It goes without saying that this loan will not be collateralized and interest rates for this type of loan will be higher than a traditional loan, regardless of your credit rating. If your home is going to have a permanent location and be on a foundation, some banks and lenders may approve a construction or mortgage loan. If your lender agrees to one of these loans, find out the specifics of the terms of the loan as they may be secured or unsecured, which will cause variation in interest rates. Also, be aware that your home must follow residential building codes and all zoning laws for your region, and be inspected and deemed fit for permanent residential housing. With these types of loans minimum square footage requirements often make tiny homes ineligible for these more traditional loans.

If your tiny home is on wheels, a recreational vehicle loan may be the way to go. To be approved for an RV loan, your tiny house must be certified and approved following the guidelines set forth by the Recreational Vehicle Industry Association. The RVIA has set regulations for health and safety requirements that cover not only the tiny house itself, but the trailer it sets on as well. Your tiny home should be deemed road worthy, and the association must certify your home. It is important to note that the RVIA will not inspect or approve any tiny house on wheels that is not manufacturer built. So, if you choose to build your tiny house yourself, you will need to seek an alternative credentialed program to inspect and certify your home.

Accrediting Agencies for THOW

Pacific West Associates, Inc. has a subsidiary named Pacific West Tiny Homes. This company is a third-party agency and is accredited. Pacific West Tiny Homes is composed of licensed professionals that includes both structural and forensic engineers, electrical engineers, and mechanical engineers. The certification and evaluation teams through this agency meet all the American Society for Testing and Materials, which is a standard for design agencies. Quality control, safety and integrity and assurance are the model for the ASTM. PWTH offers their accreditation services and provides codebooks, telephone consultations, and checklists to help ensure manufactured tiny homes are up to code and industry standards the RVIA follows.

Another company who offers similar services to DIY tiny home builders and owners is the National Association of Alternative Housing, Inc. Also, referred to as NOAH, this accreditation program is all inclusive and offers credentials and certification to manufacturers and DIY tiny home builders alike. The NOAH currently follows the guidelines set forth by the RVIA, The National Electrical Code, the National Fire Protection Agency, the American Tiny House Association Construction Association, and the National Highway & Safety Association. NOAH inspection occurs during each phase of construction to ensure compliance guidelines are met. This includes inspection of the trailer itself and all attachments, framing, electrical, HVAC, plumbing, insulation, and final inspection once construction is complete. NOAH Certification & Standard gives lenders and insurance companies the ability to underwrite equivalent values comparable to traditional permanent dwellings, and both sellers and buyers of tiny homes can access inspection records of each dwelling that is NOAH certified as all records are maintained.

Self-Financing Ideas

If you decide to finance your tiny home yourself, a tried and true method many have begun with other than dipping into their savings is to begin with a major downsize. Selling your current home and renting a small apartment or home will save you money monthly, and possibly give you the startup money you need to begin building your own home. Purging personal possessions, selling things that are not necessities, and reflecting on what you absolutely cannot live without will also give you a good idea if tiny house living is right for you. Crowd funding is also another good way to begin building your tiny house construction budget. If you have friends or family that can help you fund your dream, private loans by these means is also another option. If someone can privately fund your project, make sure that a legal agreement is met and signed by both parties, includes the terms of the person-to-person loan. Details that need to be agreed upon should include the total amount loaned, interest rates, re-payment obligations, and cover all other loan related terms.

New tiny home manufacturing companies are popping up, and if you are considering buying professional floor plans, pre-fabrication kits, or a completed home, there are many tiny house builders that will finance your purchase through their respective companies. This determination will depend upon your credit worthiness and the line of credit you need to buy their products.

Is Tiny Living Worth It?

A final financial consideration is whether tiny house living is worth it to you. Square footage for a typical tiny house range from one hundred to five hundred square feet. Before you begin to build, you need to determine how much your tiny home costs per square foot. Many people find that the actual cost of a tiny house is more than that of a traditional home, but, being that the square footage is considerably less, the tiny home will not usually cost as much as buying a regular home. The average construction cost of building a tiny home ranges around the ten-thousand-dollar range. Obviously buying top-of-the-line building materials, as opposed to building with sourced materials is a factor, but often do-it-yourself homes can easily cost $15,000-$25,000. Manufactured or professionally built homes cost on average $25,000 and up.

If you are certain that tiny house living is for you, and you have secured the finances needed to build, it is imperative that before you ever introduce hammer to nail, a secure location for the construction of your home is found. If your tiny home does not include wheels, the property wherein your home will sit needs to be secured

Michael McCord

and building permits obtained. If you are constructing a THOW in a municipality, ensuring that you are following all laws and guidelines is necessary to prevent running into any legal issues, which may cause long construction delays and going well over your budget.

Chapter 3: Zoning Laws

Zoning laws are the guidelines that govern where you can park your tiny house, whether on a foundation or on wheels. Some zoning regulations may apply to both stationary and wheeled tiny homes, while others may only apply to one or the other. Zoning laws can be tricky, especially if you choose to reside in a THOW. Each state, municipality, township, city, and county will have different zoning laws. Zoning laws can vary from county in any given state. Many zoning considerations include health and safety codes individual to each region.

Many areas require a second point of egress for tiny homes, but this may not apply to each respective home. Where you decide to park it should have an easily accessible route for any emergency vehicles. Sewer and septic hookups, how easily they are accessed by the occupants, and connection access may need to be addressed. Does your dwelling have access and use to rural, municipal, or well water? Where are the electrical hookups for your home (if needed), and are they deemed safe connections to a dwelling? Do your research on where you want to reside, and know the answers to each of these questions and what your home needs to be deemed fit for residential living.

Depending on which state you live in, some zoning laws entail and may specify a minimum or maximum size for a residence. ADU's, or alternative dwelling units are often tiny homes positioned on land that already contains a bigger permanent home. Another way to consider an ADU is as a secondary residential space on a single plot of land. A zoning consideration as far as living in your tiny home as an ADU is to be aware of the number of people that are allowed to live in one place at a time. Some cities and states govern the number of individuals allowed to live on one piece of land. If you build or park your tiny home on another's property, be aware if your home meets the zoning laws to avoid eviction.

If you choose to reside in a THOW, an RV park or trailer park may be an option for you. If your THOW is RVIA or MHBA compliant, more than likely you will have less trouble finding a place to call home, either permanently or temporarily. Another great option to consider is campgrounds. There are many campgrounds across the United States that allow not only tents and RV's, but tiny homes to stay for extended periods of time.

Essential Strategies for Seasoned Tiny House Dwellers

The ideal property for a tiny home would be private property, whether owned by yourself or another individual. Again, it is important to note that each region has different zoning laws, and that those regulations can change from not only city to city, but county by county. Not all towns have the same zoning laws that country or county property has, so knowing what is allowed where is necessary. There are new pop-up communities for tiny house living throughout America, so doing a little research can go a long way when all is said and done. Once you have picked a tentative location, call and speak to the zoning board to determine whether the location is in fact ideal. There are many places that are more than welcoming, other areas, not so much. The trick is to find where you want to go, and what zoning regulations you may run into to help prevent issues.

Here are some valuable tips on how to handle zoning boards and how to get approved easier:

- In most regions, you may be required to have property already bought and approved for the construction of a residential dwelling.

- Discuss plans with the zoning board first. Be familiar with local zoning codes. If needed, you can hire a professional to draw up a finalized set of engineered plans.

- Do not provide hand drawn plans for submission to zoning boards, as they can be seen by commission or board members as "unprofessional" and may call into question your ability to complete the build in question.

- The plans you submit should be to scale, and completely code compliant. Three copies should be made prior to meeting with zoning regulators. One copy is for you (or the builder of the structure), one copy is for the county for tax purposes, and one final copy is for the city or municipality archives. The submission should include detailed plans of egress, plumbing, electrical, structural and all mechanical topographies. The entire bill and lists of all materials used for the construction should be included in your submission as well. If any materials are not already approved by zoning guidelines, proof that they are of equal or greater quality needs to be included.

- The plans you submit for zoning approval need to show that you have adequate ventilation, moisture protection, and that all venting is a minimum of 36 inches away from windows.

- Electrical plans included in your structure need to show that your construction can handle the electrical demands placed on it by all electrical use functions, including all appliances and that those items that require dedicated circuits have them shown and labeled clearly in the plans.

- Plumbing systems should be designed to completion.

- If zoning says "no" to your project, ask what they would allow and try to get them to work with you. Overall, nearly all Building Officials are friendly, polite and there to help so I hate to admit that there are some that are downright rude. I have even seen some deny projects because they didn't fit in with the Official's vision for their jurisdiction, even though the plans complied with the zoning and municipal codes. It helps to ask local builders in your community who they recommend you work with. People in the building community will know which Officials are reasonable and which ones aren't.

- Minimum square footage allowed for residential dwellings needs to be met.

- Regional weather may dictate minimum requirements to ensure safety, including high winds, earthquakes, etc.

- Make sure to refer to city, county, and state websites and guidebooks to ensure that all health and safety codes have been met.

- Be prepared to be open to suggestion, as some zoning planners accept proposals, and send them back with changes that are needed in order for them to approve the plans you submitted. This could happen any number of times before approval is granted, so being courteous and open minded when communicating with the zoning board is important, as you may be dealing with them regularly until your proposal receives a final yes or no.

- If, despite your best efforts, your construction submission and plans are still denied, it is best to ask questions and cooperate with a professional demeanor.

- Attending council meetings to change zoning regulations in favor of tiny house living is always an option. Many regions have few to no guidelines as to what they should approve or deny. The tiny house movement is a newer one, and many laws and regulations are antiquated. If you are pleasant and persistent, your efforts may pay off. Be respectful of the people who

Essential Strategies for Seasoned Tiny House Dwellers

you are appealing to no matter how frustrated you get. Kindness always goes furthest with people.

Chapter 4: Building Codes

Building codes and guidelines is where the do-it-yourself process can get very tricky. Not impossible, but very tricky. In this chapter, we will go over how best to organize and prepare your building information to best follow building and construction guidelines set forth. It is important to reiterate that the RVIA cannot inspect nor approve a THOW that is not manufacturer built, and that NOAH or PWA are the best industry equal accrediting programs to seek guidance from.

All tiny home constructors should begin by creating a folder, file, or binder to document the entire construction process as you go. Trust me, this could save you in ways you cannot imagine in the future. The following is a list of what should be included in the construction binder:

- Original blueprints of floor plans
- Documentation as you build during each phase, including photographs

- A statement describing each individual construction method, including personal information of all individuals who helped with the construction process.

- A complete diagram of all electrical wiring.

- Photographs of framing, roof, insulation, any gas or propane lines, and plumbing.

- A complete list and bill of all materials used in construction, from the frame to the screws, including receipts for all materials. *This information may be required by the DMV where a THOW will be registered.

- A detailed illustration of the location of all joists, rafters, tension ties, hurricane clips (if used), as well as how the walls, floors, roof sections. Insulation, vapor and moisture barriers, siding, sheathing, roofing and flashing were constructed.

- Any slide out components should be approved by an engineer to guarantee safety.

- List of all chemical materials used for the interior.

If you are constructing a THOW you should know that there are load limits and specific load limits allowed to be able to tow your home.

Essential Strategies for Seasoned Tiny House Dwellers

First, your trailer must be approved to carry the weight of your home. The trailer your tiny house sits on must follow all size guidelines, and the trailer itself must also be registered with the Department of Motor Vehicle. The trailer and home must be towable by way of a bumper hitch, and the trailer needs to meet approval of the Department of Transportation standards. When considering size guidelines, be aware that height specs are measured from the bottom of the tire of the trailer, to the tallest point of your homes roof. Again, it is important to note that hauling more than 10,000 pounds may require a special license to drive.

Most building guidelines dictate a 70-square foot space as an acceptable dwelling size, and all basic daily function areas need to be accounted for, including a kitchen, bathroom, and bedroom. When framing your tiny home, high wind loads and earthquake safety guidelines need to be addressed. New, or quality building grade materials should be used when constructing your tiny house. If you are using sourced materials or found materials in your construction, each piece needs to meet the same and equal standards acceptable as if you were buying them brand new. All nails and screws, where they are used, and their purpose must

Michael McCord

meet building and construction standards and guidelines. When constructing the interior of your home, all materials must be labeled as safe for use in interiors, including paints, plastics, glues, and finishes.

A good rule of thumb when considering construction is to follow guidelines of the International Code Counsel, and their code guidebook for International Residential Codes. It is important to note, although tiny houses are not currently included within the IRC codebook, that soon may change. The ICC convened in Kentucky in April of 2016 recently and a tiny house inclusion proposal was submitted. Unfortunately, the inclusion proposal was rejected unanimously, but the tiny house inclusion was amended and resubmitted for decision for the upcoming IRC 2017 codebook. The approval, or denial of the amended proposal is set to be approved or dejected during the convenience of the ICC in October in Kansas City. This will hopefully pass, and finally create a code guideline protocol for all tiny house constructions.

Chapter 5: Maximizing Your Space

Every inch of square footage within your tiny home must be planned, organized, and utilized to maximize storage potential. Your home should be well lit and not feel overcrowded, despite the size. There are many tricks to maximize your space to its fullest potential without it feeling crowded. Aesthetics to consider that help open the space in your tiny dwelling are:

- Color and paint choices that are light in color to give the appearance of openness. Using bright whites and neutral base color pallets give the eye a feeling of expanse. Another great way to create the illusion of more space, paint interior walls and ceilings the same color.

- Strategically place mirrors and glass objects to reflect natural light into your home, and to also help reflect focal points that are pleasing to the eye.

- Use bright splashes of complementing colors throughout your home to harmonize the space while adding personal touches. Try to steer away from bold, or large prints to avoid drawing attention to tiny spaces.

- Hand window coverings above window sills to give the optical illusion of larger windows, or make sure that window coverings do not block natural light from filtering into your home. Use of sheer window treatments will help. If possible, avoiding window coverings all together may be the way to go to open the space and let the light shine in.

- Creating visual focal points that draw the eye will also help create the optical illusion of roominess. For added benefit, who is to say your focal point cannot be creative storage solutions? Shelving that is pleasing to the eye while providing function is always a good idea.

Go Vertical- Top to Bottom

To maximize your space, you need to get creative with storing your belongings. Shelving is a must, but shelf space is not the only way to store or create space on the walls.

Essential Strategies for Seasoned Tiny House Dwellers

In the Kitchen

Tiny houses mean smaller kitchens, but they do not have to mean doing without everything you need in your kitchen. Here are some space saving ideas to save time, space and money when considering the organization of your tiny kitchen:

- Instead of using cabinetry for storing pots and pans, paint a peg board, mount it to the wall, and hang kitchenware along the wall above your counterspace. This trick can also be used to hang cooking utensils.

- Rather than cluttering your tiny pantry with bulky boxes and bags of food, build a cubed shelf that hangs horizontally on the wall in the kitchen. Build the shelf to house clear plastic bins that are easily secured inside the shelf itself, and pour your pantry staples into the bins within. You have now cleared pantry shelf space, created a focal point, and have additional shelf space on the top of your shelf to house kitchen necessities.

- Retractable drawers within cabinetry or pantry storage spaces are a great alternative to traditional cabinets. Lower cabinets can have roll out or retractable drawers that house small kitchen appliances, silverware, really anything your tiny kitchen needs.

- Another option is to mount small appliances below vertical or wall hung cabinets. Microwaves can be mounted under cabinetry, and there is an emerging array of appliances that are designed to be mounted similarly, such as toasters, and can openers. Better yet, mounting magnets under cabinetry and using metal storage jars or containers frees up counter space, and is also a handy way to store knives in an easy to reach way. Placing hooks to hang mugs or lids is another great use of under cabinet space.

The point of the kitchen is function and safe storage. Make certain that there are no fire hazards, like hanging materials or objects directly over a heat source. Many people opt to enclose a hot plate in a retractable drawer as opposed to a traditional small stove, but many major appliance manufacturers produce stoves that are 24' wide or smaller. Another consideration is multifunction appliances. Three-in-one appliances that house a small toaster oven and coffee pot, and include a griddle on top offer multiple uses while using up small amounts of space.

Essential Strategies for Seasoned Tiny House Dwellers

Before completing your tiny house design, adequate storage planning is imperative. Hooks, racks, mounted storage on walls, under and in cabinets, even hanging on the inside of cabinets drawers is an easy but effective way to optimize space. Drawer organizers allowing for the safe stow-away of utensils and plates is good, but drawers can also be divided and used for food storage for potatoes, onions, or garlic as well. Your kitchen is a necessity, and needs to be one of the most detail oriented and storage-conscious planned areas in your tiny house. Consulting with a professional organizer can never hurt, but budgeting for the cost of this service is necessary.

In Common Spaces

Innovative ideas abound when considering common spaces in tiny houses. The key is to allow for multiple uses for common spaces to maximize functionality. Your living room can also function as a dining area or office space, if appropriate planning measures are taken. When considering these spaces:

- Consider furniture with multiple uses. Ottomans that add seating also can provide lidded storage, but many furniture stores offer additional versions of this, including mounted benches that are hollow, couches that include drawers below that slide out for storage, and small fold out couches can also enclose hide-a-beds for additional sleeping accommodations if you want to have guests stay over.

- Nesting tables can easily house one another, and offer an alternative workspace for anyone who needs it.

- Built in shelving that include desk spaces are a good idea, but consider a wall mounted fold down desk for workspace as well.

- Mounting televisions to a wall or within a shelving unit opens more space for foot traffic. If able, a swiveling television mount will allow for ease of viewing for many locations without the added inconvenience of actually having to relocate anything.

- Top to bottom vertical storage is important to prevent feeling claustrophobic, but it goes without saying that it is important to hide what you can. Overdoing it on open storage can make your house feel chaotic. Get creative with storage, and find the right amount of display versus store away that works for you.

- Another good idea for dividing living space without feeling cramped is to ditch formal walls completely. Using iridescent or see through materials instead of traditional walls, such as plastic or even glass, will visually open your tiny home. Dividers are an alternative to walls as well, and can offer additional display or storage of your possessions. Some may prefer to mount rods or tracks and use curtains to divide space. Whichever method you decide, make certain that functionality goes hand in hand with the look you want to achieve.

The Bedroom

Many tiny house builders opt for a loft style bedroom. If this style is for you, take advantage of the stairs leading up to the upper level.

- Hollow staircases, whether open and cubby style, or covered and including drawers, provide nooks to place things. Or, consider ditching the space stairs would take up and install a ladder on a track that moves, but be sure you are physically able to reach your bedroom. Some builders opt to install tiny stairs mounted to the wall that are less than 8' inches wide, but be sure to check building code guidelines to see what is considered safe in your region.

- Instead of a nightstand, consider installing a bedside ledge or shelf. This will allow for a place to set belongings, while saving plenty of space.

- Don't bother with a dresser in your bedroom as they are bulky, add a lot of unnecessary weight, and do not maximize storage potential. Alternatives are under-bed drawers or storage bins, shelving with bins that include dividers for smaller clothing items, or beds that are lifetable on their frames with storage provided below.

- Installing or building a Murphy bed is another great option. Murphy beds lift and sit within a built-in location in the wall, and can open your bedroom area. Newer Murphy beds can even contain shelving within the wall that rests vertically within your bed, offering storage while also ensuring protection of your shelved items if you own a THOW and want to move.

- Closet space can be tricky, but not if you plan for optimal storage. Using multiple rods for stacked hanging, or purchasing specialty hangers that fold and hand many clothing items on one are important space saving hacks. Wire racking and bin storage units can assist in storing shoes and clothing accessories. Another idea is to utilize the back of doors for hanging organizers. Or, why not ditch the closet completely? Hang rods from the ceiling to allow for hanging clothes, mounting jewelry racks or storing shoes.

The Office/ Computer Area

As mentioned previously, multi-use spaces can be located anywhere, and a home office, or electronic docking station is no different.

- Desk spaces built into the wall surrounded by shelving either along a wall or the side of another are great space savers.

- Mounting a fold down desk to a wall in another area may be enough space, but if more room is required, consider making your dining or seating area double as an at home office nook.

- Hollow shelving built into the wall creates spaces between shelves for added storage, or even mounting wooden crates stacked onto the wall with bins, baskets and storage for writing tools and other office supplies will work.

- To make travel secure and easier, consider covering your shelving or built in cabinets with a door that can not only cover the front of the shelving, but can also fold down, creating the desk space you need.

Another consideration is electrical outlets and docking stations for your phone, tablets, etc. Wherever you decide to locate your laptop, computer, or complete home office area, be certain that electrical outlets are located in a secure, safe, and convenient area. If you do not work from home, or are not in need of an entire office area, make certain that even if you nix the idea of an office in your tiny home that storage for important documents and paperwork is provided. Tiny house dwelling is all about ease, access, and living a more care-free lifestyle.

Tiny House, Tiny Bathroom

The bathroom poses some interesting complexities, but none that cannot be overcome. So, let's start with the toilet. Most tiny houses use composting toilets, but there are other options, such as:

- Standard, but smaller, flushing toilet
- RV flush toilet

Essential Strategies for Seasoned Tiny House Dwellers

- Chemical toilet

- Composting toilets offer both commercial compost styles and bucket style models

Most people opt to not install standard flushing toilets because direct access to septic systems is required, and water usage runs about five gallons for each flush. A big hole in your floor would also need to be cut out to accommodate hookup, and this may pose issues for those who opt for a tiny house on wheels. Whichever toilet you choose to install, make certain that building accommodations are acknowledged.

Installing either a free-standing sink or a tiny sized vanity sink is easy, but before you build it, consider if a second sink is necessary. Your tiny kitchen already offers a sink a few feet away. If you do choose to install a bathroom sink, a tiny vanity will offer additional chances to maximize storage that is secure.

When considering your wash station, determine whether a tiny shower will suffice, or if you cannot live without a bathtub. There are ¾ sized bathtubs available for purchase, but they aren't necessarily ¾ the price. When planning your home, keep in mind that there are many prefabricated items that can be converted and

Michael McCord

used as a tiny bathtub, if it is waterproof. An overhead or wall mounted showerhead can be installed as well, creating an untraditional, but convenient shower/tub combo.

When planning your tiny bathroom, remember to consider adequate ventilation. Mold and bacteria can ruin your hard work and effort, so be sure to do your research to discover what best suits your tiny bathroom.

Chapter 6: Tips & Tricks

As you can ascertain, tiny house living demands preparation, great organization, and attention to detail. Tiny homes need to be tailored to the owner, and all aspects of individual needs and lifestyle should be considered. These matters should be well thought out and addressed before diving in head first. Being prepared to financially fund your tiny house, build and construct or purchase your tiny home, location, and sustainable living are points to ponder.

Location, location, location

Where you want to build your tiny house, and the climate, will dictate what you need to consider when constructing or purchasing a tiny home. If you live in a northern climate, the way you heat or you're your home dictates a very different set of requirements than those located in southern regions of the America. Climate may impact:

- The type of windows you install or should have, and where in your home they are located.

- The amount and type of insulation required to keep your tiny home safe, comfortable, and efficient.

- What type of appliances you need to have, from a completely solar panel powered home, to installing a wood burning stove to keep warm?

- The utilities you have available, and all the variations.

- Heating and cooling techniques, from strategically placed windows and fans, to window or small HVAC units.

- All building materials used regarding the climate you wish to reside in.

- Ventilation, moisture control, and safety. You need to protect your investment from becoming unlivable because of mold or other issues.

Utilities

Before purchasing or building your tiny home, do your research on the variety of utilities that can be included, and determine what works best for you and where you live. You need to have a good understanding and working knowledge of each of your utilities, how they work, where they are located, and any maintenance you may need to perform on them from time to time.

Avoiding Financial Pitfalls

The best way to avoid financial calamity is to research as much as possible about tiny homes, tiny house living, and what it all entails. Get online and search for both good and bad aspects of tiny house dwelling. Before you create, purchase, or buy floor plans or an actual home and ride off into the sunset, you need to have a working understanding of all the mistakes that others have made, and then strive not to recreate them. Try to plan for everything, but prepare for anything. This includes planning and construction, zoning, building guidelines, location, and what you want to gain from transitioning into the tiny house life. Sign up with online tiny house communities and read forum and blog posts, register with tiny house associations and groups, and read everything you can get your hands on in regards to the topic and all its many aspects. While you may have your money in line to begin to build or purchase, it is always best to have an emergency or petty cash fund in the event of the inevitable, some minor mistake, error, or disaster. Trying to stay under budget on smaller aspects may free up funds for troubleshooting incidents. If all else fails and the money runs out, wait, build up additional funds, and continue when you are able.

Zone Patrol

Zoning is not always a tricky dilemma, but it often is. Sometimes becoming friendly with neighbors or coop living communities that you are zoned in is all it takes to keep the zoning board and their clip boards at bay. Other times, zoning can literally force even a seasoned tiny house dweller to abandon their home and the life they worked so hard to create for themselves and their families. Thankfully, the American Tiny House Association has created a list of state specific regions across the country that allow tiny house dwellers to either park their tiny homes on wheels, or build their tiny houses on permanent land. The most important three aspects to know about zoning in your area are:

- Is camping or parking allowed on private property (whether in urban areas or county lots), and are there time limits involved where you may need to vacate the premises?

- Are there minimum square footage requirements for new houses, either on foundations or parked on trailers?

- Does the location you wish to live allow for ADU's, that is, additional housing units on the property of homes that already exist?

- Are you prepared, both documentation wise and mentally, to petition your town or city to approve the building or parking of your tiny home in the event that zoning does not currently allow for alternative residential dwelling?

Build or Buy? That is the question!

Are you handy enough to build your own tiny house, or will you need help to achieve success? Do the floor plans and design take into consideration all the factors that need to be addressed to ensure a safe, stable, sustainable living space? If you embark on this adventure, keep in mind that while expert advice may cost extra, in the long run it can save thousands in errors. Be certain not to forget to include any professional and personal information in your build guide of anyone or any company that you advised or subcontracted with. Name, address, phone number, and any licensure or credentials may be required for approval from the municipality, zoning board, or DMV. Document every aspect of the build as you build, always take pictures, and never be ashamed to ask for help. If you are purchasing a tiny home, whether on a foundation or a trailer, ask to see proof of all credentials, approvals, and building documentation. Feel free to consider someone's background, or rates and reviews from a company you are considering purchasing from. Some companies will even provide you contact information of previous occupants so you may call and ask any questions of them. It is always best to know more than you should, than to assume every aspect of a particular home is on the up and up, simply because it is on the market for sale.

Space, Place, and Organization

Living within approximately five-hundred square feet or less can be trying at times, especially if you feel cramped or suffocated. Tiny homes have a lot less space to clean, which is great. A thing to consider however, is that without exceptional planning and organization, small spaces can easily seem cluttered and chaotic. Looking to stores that specialize in organization, or consulting with a professional organizer and

Essential Strategies for Seasoned Tiny House Dwellers

an architect may save you a lot of headache in the future, but as always, you need to budget for it. Many pictures of tiny house space saving techniques abound on the internet, so save pictures of good ideas or things to try. If you decide to consult with a professional, or just a friend or family member who is familiar with the processes, bring your ideas and photographs with you to reference them.

Chapter 7: Insurance

Insuring Tiny Homes

Now, insuring your tiny house may not be required, and it can be a very taxing accomplishment to achieve, but consider if all your worldly possessions went up in flames, and you had no financial nest egg to replace it all. You could be facing complete ruin. There are different scenarios for insuring tiny homes, and we will be discussing the different factors next.

Insurance During Building

Builders insurance policies cover the structure you are building during the construction process. Bear in mind, many insurance under-writers will only offer builders insurance policies if a licensed professional builder or construction company is doing the project, and the professionals are bonded. That being said, it does not hurt to speak with your insurance agent to see if a policy like this is possible to attain anyways, as minimum size requirements may allow the agent to cover the structure during the build phase as an out building similar to a shed.

Tiny homes on foundations

If you decided to purchase a tiny home that Is prefabricated, your insurance headache may be minimal. Many tiny house manufacturers build their homes to be RVIA compliant, and meet Federal Safety Standard guidelines. These homes are already certified by an accredited program. Most manufacturers offer their own insurance providers, so it is simply a matter of signing up for your insurance and paying the premium set forth. Keep in mind, that if you decided to do-it-yourself, your tiny home will be harder to insure, whether it is stationary and setting on a foundation or a tiny house on wheels.

Insurance Protection During Moving your Tiny Home

If your tiny house is built in a location other than where it will sit permanently and will need to be towed to its permanent location, it may be possible to insure the trip. Trip or travel insurance may be preferred, or required by the Department of Transportation. Both the DOT and the insurance provider view the home itself as a load on a trailer, or a haul. The trailer the home rests on is a separate issue and will require

Essential Strategies for Seasoned Tiny House Dwellers

a separate insurance policy through your automotive insurance carrier. There may be issued involved with getting your home to its final destination, so one option is to hire a towing or moving company to haul your home for you. Towing companies are fully insured in their own right, and hiring someone to do the moving for you is much less stressful than other means, but can cost quite a bit.

If you choose to haul your tiny home yourself, there may be some loopholes your insurance agent can use to help you get insured and on the road. One such insurance tactic is to issue a commercial trucking insurance policy. This type of policy allows the insurance company to categorize your tiny home and the towing of it the same way other companies can haul modular homes down the highway, but, there is a catch: Commercial trucking policies are for the movers of other people's property, and cannot be approved for the owner of the home. Here is a way around that major detail:

- Ask a friend or family member to temporarily buy your home.

- Secure a professional appraisal from a licensed builder of the market value of your home.

- Draw up a bill of sale, details need to include complete sale terms of the home including a down-payment, and conditions for final payment to be received upon delivery of the home.

- Include copies of payment receipts.

- Both parties need to sign all documentation of the sale of the home, and the documentation needs to be notarized.

Now, you are no longer the owner of the property that needs to be hauled or towed (wink wink), and you are eligible to qualify for a commercial trucking insurance policy. This process may seem like one giant headache, but it is fair to say that it is a much more cost effective way than hiring a towing or moving company, especially if your tiny home will be travelling a longer distance.

THOW Insurance

Insuring a tiny house on wheels is much more difficult than insuring stationary homes, but it is possible! As mentioned previously, your auto insurance carrier will provide the insurance for the trailer your home rests on, the issue is with finding a way to insure the home that sets upon it. Some insurance companies may compare tiny houses on wheels to long-term recreational vehicles or travel trailers. If your tiny home is certified via RVIA methods and meets the criteria, a policy in that vein can be attained if your house meets all National Highway Safety Standards and is built to code and guidelines that apply. Certification of your THOW through other programs, such as NOAH or PWA may be accepted by the under-writer as well, but that is dependent upon the agent you work with, and what the company standards and policies are.

Located in Portland, Oregon, Darrell Granz Insurance, a local insurance provider, has collaborated with Lloyds of London to develop a policy that specifically covers tiny homes (both mobile and stationary) and is so far, the only market supplier to delve into this respective market. Considering that Oregon is one of the states currently leading the trends involved with the tiny house movement, it is no surprise that a company is answering the call of an emerging need. This newly developed policy offers coverage to your tiny house that covers the market value of your tiny dwelling, as well as the possessions contained within in the event of fire. Premium rates are averaged at around $500 per year, and the yearly premium is due up front, as no financing is offered on this package. Previously only offered to tiny homes that resided in Washington, Nevada, Oregon, Utah, Arizona, and Colorado, this insurance package was recently made available to tiny houses in all states. The policy costs do range, especially if you live in rural areas and emergency response times may be greater due to location in a more remote area. It is important to note that theft, and loss during travel along highways is not covered under this policy.

Renters Insurance

Renters insurance policy coverage is the easiest way to go for most tiny home owners. These policies are fairly easy to obtain, but some monthly premiums cost more than with other carriers. Shopping around to find the best quote to fit your needs is strongly suggested. Renters insurance will cover all the possessions within your tiny house, and may also include personal liability. Personal liability clauses cover you in the event someone sustains an injury while in or on your tiny home. Renters insurance underwriters seem to be working with tiny home owners, but it is important to note that THOW owners do tend to run into more issues, as under-writers may not be able to ensure a

Essential Strategies for Seasoned Tiny House Dwellers

THOW as it may not follow their company's standards or definitions of permanent residential dwellings, and may not be built to their housing standards.

A final and very important reminder when mulling over your insurance needs and research efforts: For almost any insurance carrier to agree to cover your tiny home, a complete electrical inspection is often mandatory. General inspections are often required.

Chapter 8:
Tiny Homes Big Communities

The total tiny house living movement is based on the idea of community, freedom, and a more basic way of life. Decreasing the price of basic necessities such as rent or mortgage, largely reduced cost of utilities, and the ability some dream of to be able to move at will are also very appealing. The bonus of creating a closer-knit feeling and atmosphere of community only makes tiny house living that much more appealing.

There are certainly those that wish to live unattached that can afford to do so, but tiny homes also offer a frugal and safe alternative for those less fortunate. There are many tiny home communities that currently exist for the sole purpose of providing shelter for the less-fortunate, as well as many being planned or developed currently. Below is a list of tiny home communities, where they are located, and what amenities they offer, including the demographics of each listed.

- Lux Tiny Community in Pinetop-Lakeside in Arizona is placed on 6 acres. There will be 45 spaces offered for rent with rental prices fluctuating from $329-$359 monthly.

- The Lavra is a community in rural California, sited between San Luis Obispo and Arroyo Grande. This community partakes in farming activities. Another village in California is Lemon Cove Village. Lemon Cove is in northern California, and is a tiny home society that was once an RV park. Rent for a lot runs between $450-$595 per month, and contains access to all common areas for a fee. In Nevada City, California the Ingenium Expressive Arts Village that is at present being developed, is expected to open in fall of 2017

- Located in Fairplay, Colorado, Whispering Aspen Village is the start of a tiny house village that is subsidized by a tiny home RV manufacturer. Lots, including tiny homes will range from $29,000 to $39,900. Further developers are also scheduling to build communities in Salida and Walsenburg.

- The city of Rockledge, Florida has just approved the building of a tiny house community for both tiny houses on foundations and tiny houses on wheels will be welcome once completed. Orlando currently accommodates a lakefront tiny house community and RV park that is open year-round called the Orlando Lakefront at College Park

- Guyton, Georgia is home to Green Bridge Farm, that is balanced around a twenty-year-old organic farm. This supportable community is located on wooded acres, with the farm is a community space. For $300 a month, you can lease small lots to place your THOW with electricity provided.

- The Abundance Ecovillage Project in Fairfield, Iowa is placed on 15 acres fewer than 3 miles from town. This intentional tiny house community focuses on renewable energy and green living. Many communal spaces include a community garden, outdoor theatre, ponds, and hiking. Although not required, residents prefer biking rather than the use of automobile transportation to reduce their carbon footprint.

- Lomax Tiny House Community in Indiana is designed as a gated, high-end community for tiny houses on wheels.

Plots come with well water access, electricity, and septic utilities. Towering Pines Vineyard is also located in Indiana, and shortly the vineyard will welcome the expansion of tiny house lots. This setting includes a learning center and an organic farm.

- Cottage Estates is a tiny house community that is also supported by a manufacturer, and located within Travers Bay RV Resort in Williamsburg, Michigan. This community is also an upmarket community.

- Ogilvie, Minnesota is home to The Sanctuary Minnesota, an 80-acre community that is home to two tiny houses that are rentable, and contain six places to park tiny homes on wheels. This community is not for children, and cats are presently the only pets allowed on the premises.

- Truly Green Energy Worker's Cooperative Village is in Yaak, Montana, and is comprised of a central kitchen and dining hall, four businesses, and is geared towards globally minded individuals.

Essential Strategies for Seasoned Tiny House Dwellers

- There are intentional communities that accept tiny houses in both Missouri and New Mexico. Cavallos de las Estrallas is an eco-resort and tiny house community that is currently under development in Rodeo, New Mexico.

- Llamalopolis set in the Fremont East area of Las Vegas, Nevada. Also referred to as Airstream Park, the community welcomes visitors and new members by invitation only as it is owned by the CEO of a popular internet based company, so trying to get yourself invited may be tricky.

- North Carolina is a great state with tiny home living in mind. Highland Lake Cove in Flat Rock offers land obtainable for lease, and welcomes tiny homes. Another community located in Flat Rock, The Village of Wildflowers was originated on the "smaller IS better" opinion and is home to many tiny homes for rent or purchase. High Cove is in a country area of Mitchell County. In Kernersville and Chapel Hill, two additional tiny housing community developments are at present being developed and built.

- If Ohio sounds appealing, the town of De Graff is home to a gorgeous orchard and collective farm situated on seven acres of land and offers plots for six tiny houses.

- Being one of the first states to pioneer the tiny house drive, Oregon is extremely tiny house friendly. The city of Portland is home to Simply Home Community, which contains the site of a consulting business that specializes in tiny houses. The city has also proposed and accepted the erection of micro-communities, and these lively neighborhood developments are encouraged by city leaders and officials. The foundation behind micro-communities is to deliver safe, affordable housing geared towards the working poor, or those that live near or beneath the poverty line. The planning of these micro-communities includes collective spaces and a supportive feel. Dignity Village is also located in Portland and is an official homeless base camp that offers internet access, counselling, and education services for the homeless and disabled population. Formerly an old RV park, Lakeview Tall Town Tiny Village is a developing tiny home community that offers rental or purchase lots, but utilities cost extra.

- Texas is also developing and building tiny home communities. Austin Live|Work is a 10-acre land development that has tiny house owners in mind. Community First! Village is also a prearranged tiny house community that is currently under progress in Austin. Situated on 27 acres, the goal of this community is to provide affordable residential houses to the disabled, homeless, and underserved populace. Tiny houses, mobile homes, and RV's are included in the development. In Willis, Texas, a tiny home expansion us underway at Healing Hands Ranch that will be available and welcome the general population, but will also be made available to the inhabitants of Healing Hands Ranch.

- Cabot, Vermont is home to the Headwaters Garden & Learning Center, and is a green living village that welcomes tiny homes.

- Quixote Village in Olympia, Washington was once a homeless tent camp. Now, it is the home to thirty tiny homes on foundations and consists of many common spaces for its inhabitants, including laundry facilities, showers, and dining areas.

This is not a complete list of every tiny house community in the United States, and more are being planned and erected at this time. Looking to the internet, you can find similar communities that welcome tiny houses and their owners in almost every state.

Chapter 9: Harmony, Green Living, & Places to Park

Community Equals Harmony

The whole rationalization for choosing to live in a tiny dwelling is that it forces you to liberate yourself of a huge quantity of your belongings. Consequently, many people find themselves somewhat reliant on the community and the neighbors that reside within in times of need. Storage is limited to each tiny homeowner, so many members of these intentional living neighborhoods find themselves having to share tools and many other items, to pool their resources in order to make sure that everyone has everything they need. This type of shared property and possessions helps to instill a sense of belonging among the inhabitants, and many of these communities lean toward a more co-operative system.

Many tiny districts create almost a society all their own, and many enjoy common spaces. The purpose of these common spaces is to create a neutral area within the community wherein people will naturally congregate, social interactions invariably take place, and associations, alliances, and connections take form. While individual goals or wishes are accomplished, community fostering and increased socialization also emerge, predominantly if people share work on a venture or purpose. Individual benefits occur unsurprisingly, improved public well-being, and social resilience are possible positive results.

There are many benefits to communal living, one being the co-op gardens many micro-communities have on site. There are many health rewards, as community gardening gets individuals outdoors, and physically moving. The idea that this is how the individuals and the neighbors all eat is great motivator in getting everyone that resides within the community to participate. This common space not only encourages interpersonal relationships among the dwellers to accomplish a common goal, it also helps initiate physical fitness which also translates into happier people. Also, sharing a common goal creates a sense of belonging among everyone involved.

The tiny community is more than just minimizing and paring down, it is clearly about including everyone in something bigger than just the individual. The psychological benefits of connecting to other people, and relying on each other is a powerful and positive way to enhance overall happiness. Communities that offer common dining spaces give the residents a chance to break bread together, and become acquainted with each other in a non-pressured atmosphere. Cooking meals together, and eating with one another encourages a sense of togetherness, even family. This encouraged sense of belonging only helps satisfy our human need to create bonds with other people.

Green Living and the Bigger Picture

Reducing ones overall mass of material objects can be very freeing, but how does tiny house living help the environment really? It a lot of ways, actually. The average size of a house has increased in size by almost sixty percent over the last 40 years. Bigger homes being built equal less land for everyone, less spaces for natural and planned vegetation to grow...and we all know trees help clear our air and food has to be grown to be eaten.

Structures, that is homes and buildings, account for about 70% of the United States electricity usage, and almost 40% of all carbon dioxide emissions are perpetrated but structures, not cars, and almost 20% of our green-house gas emissions in America are produced by residential homes.

Our forests are in jeopardy too. New construction projects, especially for average size homes and new businesses are eating away the earth's tree population much more than many realize. The wood used to build just one 3,000 square foot home would stretch four miles if it were lain end-to-end. Roughly ¾ of all lumber used in America is used to build these exact type of projects. The sheer mass of regular or large sized building projects contributes around twenty to upwards of forty percent of our nations solid waste stream. When building your tiny home, please consider visiting local wood suppliers, as many offer wasted wood to individuals for sell at a cheaper rate, and many will give the free lumber away to avoid having to deal with the waste or disposal.

Tiny homes are easily heated, cooled, and can even be completely powered using alternative energy. Solar panels can be attached directly to a tiny house, or can be stored within a THOW and set outdoors once a destination is reached. The often used composting toilets, the use of alternative water sources, all only help decrease the carbon footprint, and encourage a planet friendly way of living. Some tiny homes have the capacity to use only rainwater collection and filtration techniques, completely eliminating the cost and waste associated to regular municipal water sources. The tiny house movement is a way that we as a whole can help create a return to environmentally conscious living, while still maintaining all the modern conveniences that we all enjoy today.

Places to Park

If you are looking for places to park a tiny home on wheels throughout the United States, the list below is a great place to start. Keep in mind that while these locations have been verified as tiny house friendly, contacting the camping ground operators prior to showing up to ask questions or make reservations is a good idea to ensure that your THOW meets park guidelines. This list is in no way a complete list of locations that allow tiny houses, and many other campsites and parks will be more than happy to accomodate tiny home owners. Again, contacting any location prior to visiting is always a good idea.

Michael McCord

Arizona

- Tucson: Voyager RV Park – 8701 S Kolb Road, Tucson, AZ

California

- Palm Springs: Horizon Mobile Village & RV Park – 3573 East Palm Canyon Drive, Palm Springs, CA

Colorado

- Woodland: Peak View Park – 19253 US Hwy 24, Woodland Park, CO

Florida

- Orlando: Orlando Lakefront at College Park – 3405 N Orange Blossom Trail, Orlando, FL

Georgia

- Warthen: Warthen RV Park – 9470 S. Sparta Davisboro Rd, Warthen, GA

Illinois

- Sesser: Old Bates Campground – 5272 Peach Orchard Road, Sesser, IL. Call 618-625-6250 or email geegees@yahoo.com

Iowa

- Monticello: Walnut Acres Campground – 22128 Highway 38 North, Monticello, IA

Kansas

- Mulvane: – Mulvane Mobile Home & RV Park, 1455 N Webb Rd, Mulvane, KS. Contact: gotadvantage@gmail.com

Louisiana

- Slidell: New Orleans East Kampground – 56009 Hwy 433 in Slidell, LA

Maryland

- College Park: Cherry Hill Park – 9800 Cherry Hill Road, College Park, MD

Maine

- Scarborough: Bailey's Camping Resort – 275 Pine Point Road, Scarborough, ME

Minnesota

- Knife River: Knife River Campground – 196 Scenic Drive, Knife River, MN

Michael McCord

Nevada

- Las Vegas: Airstream Park, part of the Downtown Project, 1001 Fremont Street, Las Vegas, NV

New Hampshire

- Brookline: Field & Stream RV Park – 7 Dupaw Gould Road, Brookline, NH

New Jersey

- Cream Ridge: Timberland Lake Campground – 1335 Reed Road, Cream Ridge, NJ

New Mexico

- New Communities: River Edge Mobile Home Park – Rio Communities, NM

New York

- Queensbury: Lake George Campsites – 1053 Route 9, Queensbury, NY

North Carolina

- Asheville: Wilson's Riverfront RV Park – 225 Amboy Road, Asheville, NC

Ohio

- Swanton – Hidden Lake Campground – 6435 S. Fulton Lucas Rd, Swanton, OH. Open year round. Tiny houses must be self-contained. Call Stephanie at 419-875-5476.

Oregon

- Portland: Sauvie Island Cove RV Park – 31421 NW Reeder Road, Portland, OR

Pennsylvania

- Burnt Cabins: Ye Olde Mill Campground – 582 Grist Mill Road, Burnt Cabins, PA

Rhode Island

- Pascoag: Echo Lake Campground – 200 Moroney Road, Pascoag, RI. Open seasonally May through September. No pets allowed.

South Carolina

- Aiken: Pine Acres Campground – 205 Duke Drive, Aiken, SC.

Michael McCord

Texas

- Corsicana: American RV Park Corsicana has a designated area for tiny houses – 4345 West Highway 31, Corsicana, TX

Utah

- Moab: Moab Valley RV Resort & Campground – 1773 US 191, Moab, UT

Virginia

- Bowling Green: Hidden Acres Family Campground – 17391 Richmond Turnpike, Milford at Bowling Green, VA

Washington

- Castle Rock: Toutle River Resort – 150 Happy Trails, Castle Rock, WA

Wisconsin

- Lodi: Smokey Hollow Campground – W9935 McGowan Road, Lodi, WI. Open seasonally, from April to October.

Conclusion

Thank for purchasing Tiny House Living: Essential Strategies for Seasoned Tiny House Dwellers. We hope that we have provided you with intermediate level information to help you in your quest to live the tiny house lifestyle unconstrained. The goal is to live the life you want, and making it easier by providing you with the tools, tricks, and tips to avoid many errors that can easily occur when completely transforming the way you live.

The next step is to consider all the information provided you, and get ready to make the move to a better, simpler way of life.

Finally, if you found this book useful in anyway, a review on Amazon is always appreciated!

CPSIA information can be obtained
at www.ICGtesting.com
Printed in the USA
BVHW042124120122
626124BV00015B/442